D0607378

A VISUAL LEARNER'S GUIDE TO BEING A GROWN-UP

MATT SHIRLEY

RUNNING PRESS

PHILADELPHIA

Copyright © 2021 by Matt Shirley
Cover copyright © 2021 by Hachette Book Group, Inc.

Hachette Book Group supports the right to free expression and the value of copyright. The purpose of copyright is to encourage writers and artists to produce the creative works that enrich our culture.

The scanning, uploading, and distribution of this book without permission is a theft of the author's intellectual property. If you would like permission to use material from the book (other than for review purposes), please contact permissions@hbgusa.com. Thank you for your support of the author's rights.

Running Press
Hachette Book Group
1290 Avenue of the Americas, New York, NY 10104
www.runningpress.com
@Running_Press

Printed in China

First Edition: April 2021

Published by Running Press, an imprint of Perseus Books, LLC, a subsidiary of Hachette Book Group, Inc. The Running Press name and logo is a trademark of the Hachette Book Group.

The Hachette Speakers Bureau provides a wide range of authors for speaking events. To find out more, go to www.hachettespeakersbureau.com or call (866) 376-6591.

The publisher is not responsible for websites (or their content) that are not owned by the publisher.

Print book cover and interior design by Susan Van Horn.

Library of Congress Control Number: 2020944246

ISBNs: 978-0-7624-9997-7 (hardcover), 978-0-7624-9995-3 (ebook)

RRD-S

10 9 8 7 6 5 4 3 2 1

CONTENTS

INTRODUCTION

ABOUT FIVE YEARS AGO, I DECIDED THAT I WAS TIRED OF TRYING TO BE AN ADULT—dealing with corporate lingo, resetting my passwords no less than twenty times in one month, and constantly coming up with excuses to cancel plans I didn't want in the first place—I was over it. Like many, my attention span shortened to that of an infant's so I sought out different ways to convey my daily frustrations with being a grown-up. The answer, as you may have guessed by now, was charts.

I think charts are great because they don't require a bunch of reading and there is an inherent "figuring it out" component that gives the reader a sense of accomplishment. Plus, there are colors and stuff. And in the internet age, no one wants to spend more than a few seconds looking at something anyway.

So, one day I decided over a boring cup of coffee one boring afternoon at a boring office job that I would try to make a chart every day on a whiteboard. I didn't have any grand plans in mind; I just wanted to see if I could do it—and maybe make a couple of my Instagram followers chuckle along the way.

And then, like one of those dinosaur sponges that you put in water as a kid, the idea grew. I put some of my charts on Reddit and they went to the front page. Then some websites started to write about me and I got a lot more followers. I figured out that, yup, people liked charts.

What follows is a collection of 118 charts, visuals, tables, and graphs that's like a journey through the major steps of adulthood—from work, sex, aging, and friendship, to dealing with your slow-witted friends and insane family. My goal here isn't to change your point of view on these topics, or even to convince you that it will all get better. I just want to make it clear that you're not in this alone.

Maybe we can navigate this together and come out on the other side feeling a little more grown up. Or maybe, if you don't feel like doing much growth right now, you can just sit back, relax, and enjoy the pretty pictures.

WORK

My first job was at a pool store, dusting hot tubs and testing swimming pool water incorrectly over the summers of my sophomore and junior years of high school. I earned a cool $4.25 an hour. Oh, how I longed for my lunch breaks, where I would get spicy chicken strips and a Dr Pepper from the KFC next door, if only because destroying my tongue with a sodium burn gave me something to do with my afternoons. Each hour, I would tally up how much I had made so far that day—$4.25, $8.50, $12.75—and each hour I would be disappointed in how not rich I was becoming. It was my first foray into paid work and the first time I asked myself, "Is this really worth it?"

Flash-forward many years, where I found myself in a conference room at a corporate headquarters of a real company and I had the same question banging around in my head. Throughout the hiring process and all the meetings I had to attend and all the emails I pretended to read, I learned a lot, but none of it was what they were trying to teach me. What I actually learned was that all of this work that we do day in and day out is ripe to be ridiculed. So let's get on with that ridicule, shall we?

USING THE WORK BATHROOM

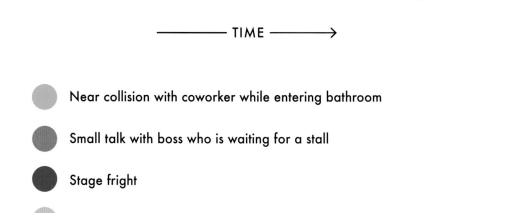

TIME ⟶

 Near collision with coworker while entering bathroom

Small talk with boss who is waiting for a stall

 Stage fright

The reason you came to the bathroom

Making eye contact with people through the stall cracks

Washing your hands extra long so you don't have to go back to your desk

 Near collision with coworker while exiting bathroom

EXPERIENCE REQUIRED

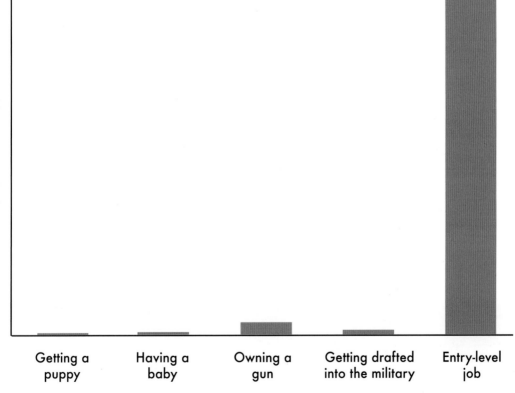

AMOUNT OF EXPERIENCE REQUIRED

Getting a puppy | Having a baby | Owning a gun | Getting drafted into the military | Entry-level job

WHAT KIND OF OFFICE WORKER

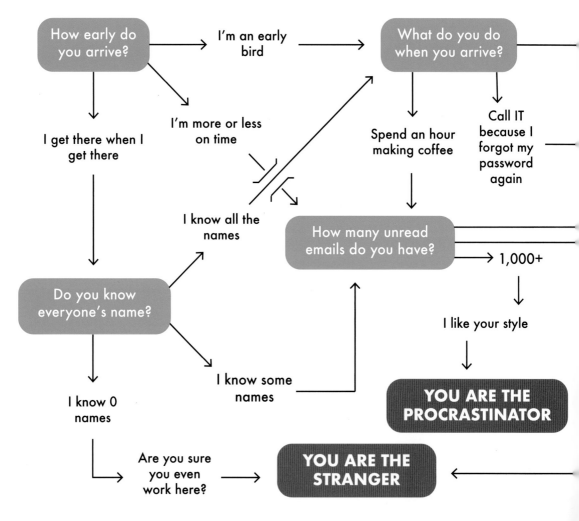

ARE YOU?

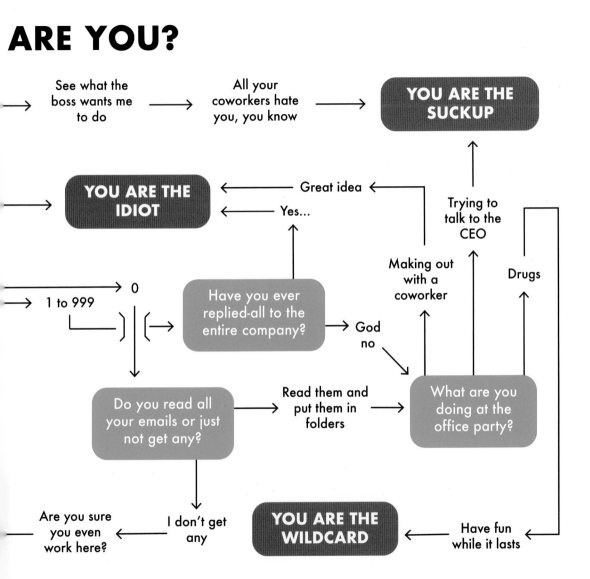

See what the boss wants me to do → All your coworkers hate you, you know →

YOU ARE THE SUCKUP

Great idea ←

YOU ARE THE IDIOT

Yes... ←

Trying to talk to the CEO

Making out with a coworker

Drugs

0

1 to 999

Have you ever replied-all to the entire company?

God no

What are you doing at the office party?

Do you read all your emails or just not get any?

Read them and put them in folders →

Are you sure you even work here? ←

I don't get any

YOU ARE THE WILDCARD

Have fun while it lasts

THE FIRST DAY OF A NEW JOB

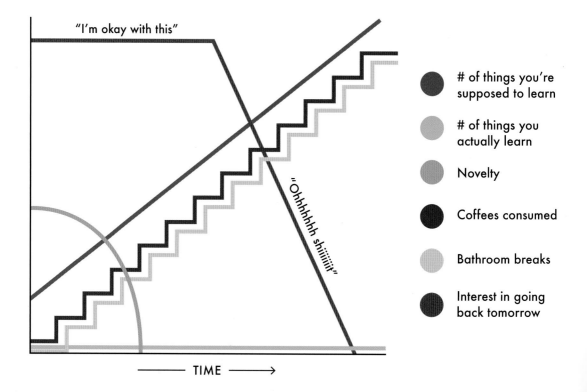

"I'm okay with this"

"Ohhhhhh shiiiiit"

- # of things you're supposed to learn
- # of things you actually learn
- Novelty
- Coffees consumed
- Bathroom breaks
- Interest in going back tomorrow

TIME →

CORPORATE LINGO TRANSLATOR

TERM	TRANSLATION
Salaried position	You'll work overtime but not earn overtime
Flexible lunches	You'll work at your desk over lunch
Unlimited vacation	No vacation
Summer half-day Fridays	Autumn full-day Saturdays
Unlimited breaks	No breaks
Company computer and phone	You can't watch porn on them you know
Flexible schedules	As long as you're working every waking moment
Traveling opportunities	You will be living in hotel rooms and forget your kids' names
Work-from-home opportunities	The office is your home now
Advancement opportunities	Absolutely! (You're going to need to murder your boss, though)

TYPICAL WORK WEEK

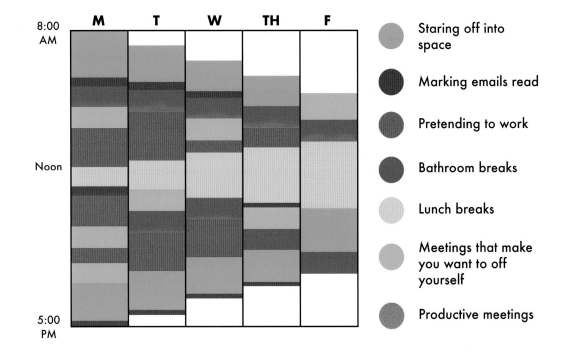

8:00 AM	M	T	W	TH	F

- Staring off into space
- Marking emails read
- Pretending to work
- Bathroom breaks
- Lunch breaks
- Meetings that make you want to off yourself
- Productive meetings

ZOOM CALL TIMELINE

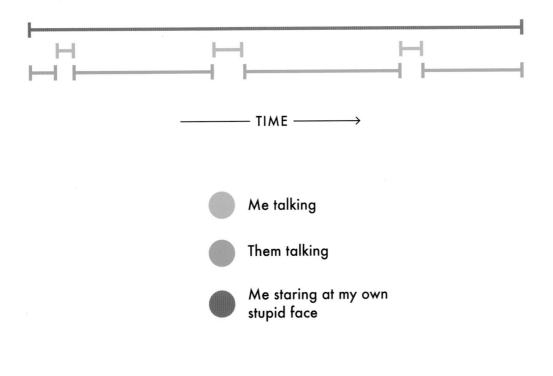

TIME

Me talking

Them talking

Me staring at my own stupid face

RESETTING YOUR PASSWORD

Please choose a new password

Sorry, password must be at least 12 characters long

Sorry, password must include at least one uppercase letter, one number, and one special character

Sorry, password must include at least one hieroglyph and one algebraic equation

Sorry, password must include at least one bible verse and one pejorative slur

Sorry, password must include at least one Civil War general and Stuart Little's inseam

Sorry, password cannot be a password you've used before

COMPLETING A TASK

WHAT YOU SHOULD DO	WHAT YOU ACTUALLY DO
Break it into little steps	Think of it as a giant, overwhelming, impenetrable mass
Aim for completion, not perfection	Spend two hours deciding whether or not you need that comma
Choose a productive environment	Don't leave bed
Get rid of distractions	The TV, phone, and 195 opened tabs aren't distractions, right?
Find a work buddy	Find a drinking buddy
Create a detailed timeline	It's due in 15 minutes so you have 15 minutes
Take a deep breath	Panic
Outline your goals	Realize that the task has no purpose, much like your life
Just do it already	Just don't do it, ever

13

WORK EMAIL

B I N G O

Accidental reply all	Reply all to be removed from reply all thread	"Cheers!"	Inspirational quote in signature	Email sent to wrong Matt/Haley/John/Jess
FWD: FWD: FWD:	300-word email in one long sentence	Guy who still double spaces after periods	Second-grade writing level	HR email about dirty kitchen
"Sorry just saw this"	Out of office reply still on after vacation ends	FREE SPACE CC's boss on everything	"There's free useless garbage in the break room"	Fantasy football invite
Unsolicited baby photos	Your/you're mistake	Forgot to attach attachment	Forgot it again in follow up email	"Let's touch base next week"
"I'm going to be thirty seconds late to meeting"	Five emails that could have been one email	Girl who emails entire company about dentist appointment	Google doc invite	Email about too many emails

EVERY MEETING SEATING CHART EVER

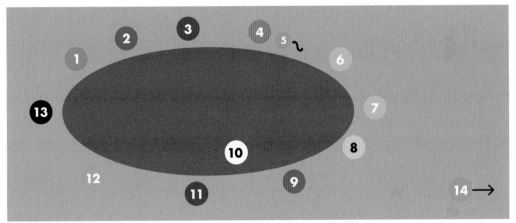

1	You	9	Guy with just the worst ideas
2	Ice-cruncher	9	But also talks the most
3	Guy who only talks in questions?	10	Office drunk
4	Girl who has a "service" dog	11	19 sneezes in a row girl
5	Dog that just peed in the corner	12	Eating microwaved fish for some reason
6 7	Couple who just had a terribly awkward breakup	13	Your boss's boss (who hates you)
8	Captain Interrupto	14	Where you'd like to be

PUBLIC SPEAKING

EXPECTATION

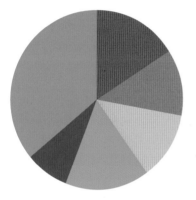

REALITY

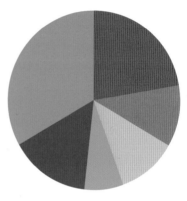

EXPECTATION

- Sharing interesting anecdotes
- Telling hilarious jokes
- Asserting confident rebuttals
- Answering questions from a captive audience
- Introspection
- Opening minds and creating crushes

REALITY

 Sweating

 Not remembering what you're supposed to say next

 Not remembering what you just said

 Sipping from an already empty bottle

 Panicked stuttering

Putting people to sleep and crushing dreams

WORKING FROM HOME

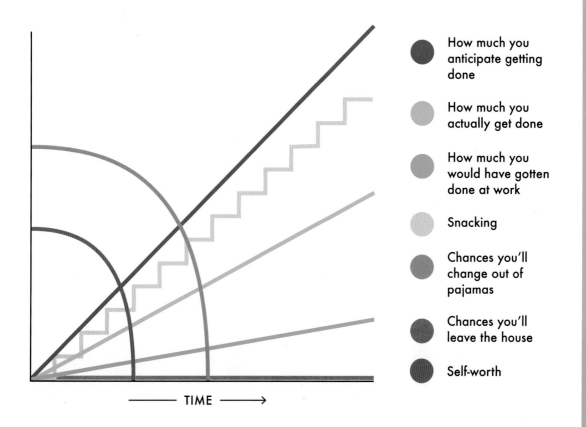

- How much you anticipate getting done
- How much you actually get done
- How much you would have gotten done at work
- Snacking
- Chances you'll change out of pajamas
- Chances you'll leave the house
- Self-worth

TIME

MODERN PROFESSIONALS: DECODED

JOB TITLE	WHAT IT ACTUALLY MEANS
Real estate agent	Professional hot person
Uber driver	Professional traffic
Politician	Professional liar
Server	Professional asshole neutralizer
YouTube star	Professional asshole
Screenwriter	Professional unemployed person
Unemployed person	Professional worrier
Most everyone else	Professional email checker

JOB EXCITEMENT LEVELS

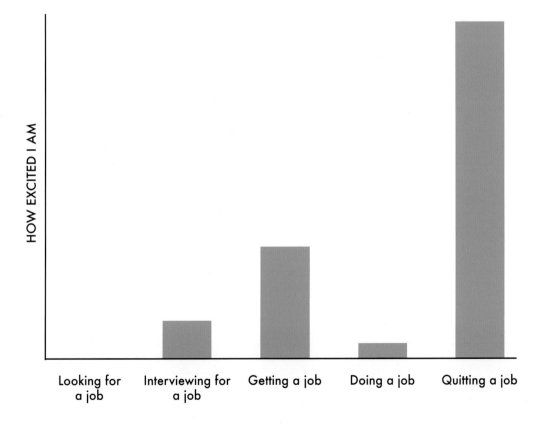

HOW EXCITED I AM

Looking for a job | Interviewing for a job | Getting a job | Doing a job | Quitting a job

SOCIALIZING AND LEISURE

Ah, leisure—the thing we do when we aren't working or sleeping or dealing with our family or grooming ourselves or going on dates or dealing with our other family or losing our minds. In other words, the thing we almost never do.

I have to be honest with you here: I'm not very good at leisure. And I'm even less good at socializing. Something about all those years of being locked up in a tiny house with my three brothers probably has something to do with it. I always thought leisure was the thing you did to get away from your family. And these days, it feels like leisure is the thing you do to get away from reality.

But that's not to say there aren't things we can do to unwind, relax, and have a little fun. For example, watching thousands of hours of television!

HOBBIES

WHAT I SAY I LIKE TO DO

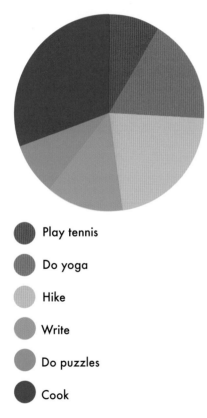

- Play tennis
- Do yoga
- Hike
- Write
- Do puzzles
- Cook

WHAT I ACTUALLY LIKE TO DO

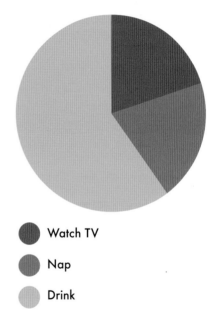

- Watch TV
- Nap
- Drink

BOWLING

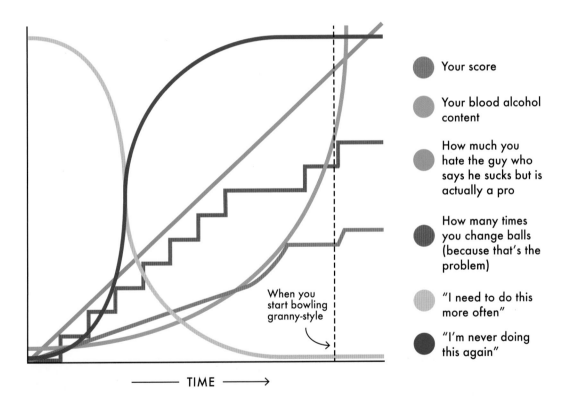

- Your score
- Your blood alcohol content
- How much you hate the guy who says he sucks but is actually a pro
- How many times you change balls (because that's the problem)
- "I need to do this more often"
- "I'm never doing this again"

When you start bowling granny-style

TIME

CANCELING PLANS EXCUSE GENERATOR

CHOOSE AN INTRO	+	CHOOSE A SCAPEGOAT	+	CHOOSE A DELAY
Sorry I can't come		my nephew		just shit the bed
Please forgive my absence		the ghost of Hitler		died in front of me
This is going to sound crazy but		the Pope		won't stop telling me knock knock jokes
Get this:		my ex		is having a nervous breakdown
I can't go because		a high school marching band		gave me syphilis
I know you're going to hate me but		Dan Rather		poured lemonade in my gas tank
I was minding my own business and boom!		a sad clown		stabbed me
I feel terrible but		the kid from Air Bud		found my box of human teeth
I regretfully cannot attend,		a professional cricket team		stole my bicycle
This is going to sound like an excuse but		my Tinder date		posted my nudes on Instagram

HGTV SHOWS

WHAT SHE WANTS   vs.   **WHAT HE WANTS**

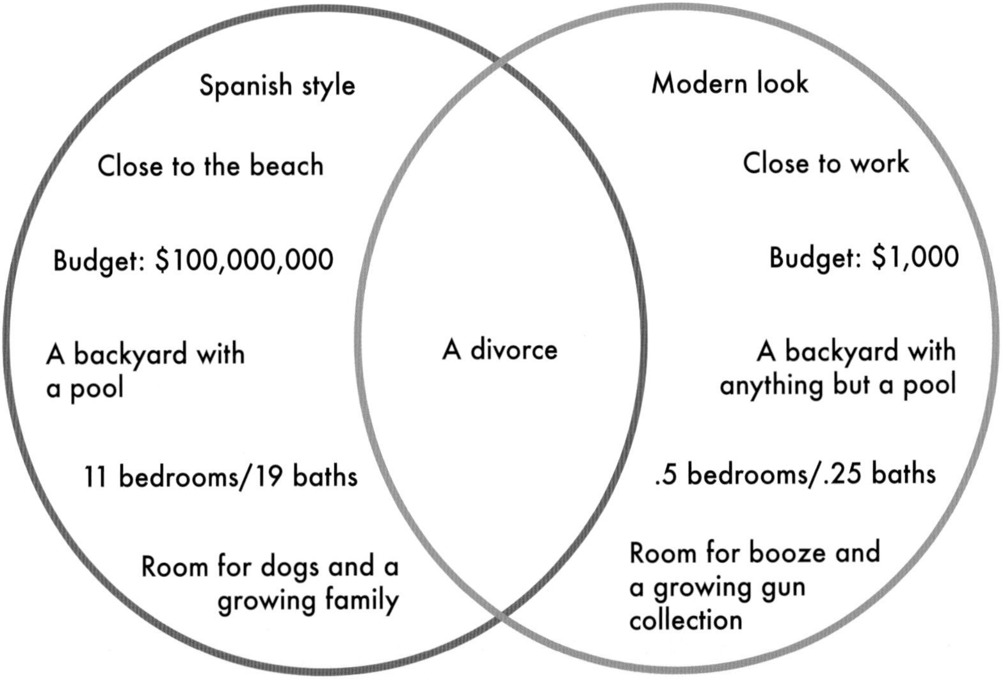

Spanish style

Close to the beach

Budget: $100,000,000

A backyard with
a pool

A divorce

11 bedrooms/19 baths

Room for dogs and a
growing family

Modern look

Close to work

Budget: $1,000

A backyard with
anything but a pool

.5 bedrooms/.25 baths

Room for booze and
a growing gun
collection

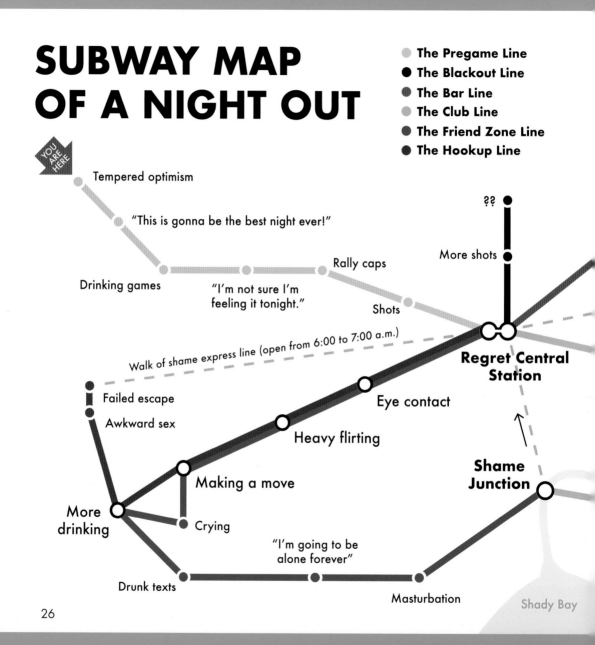

SUBWAY MAP OF A NIGHT OUT

- The Pregame Line
- The Blackout Line
- The Bar Line
- The Club Line
- The Friend Zone Line
- The Hookup Line

YOU ARE HERE

Tempered optimism

"This is gonna be the best night ever!"

Drinking games

"I'm not sure I'm feeling it tonight."

Rally caps

Shots

??

More shots

Walk of shame express line (open from 6:00 to 7:00 a.m.)

Regret Central Station

Failed escape

Awkward sex

Eye contact

Heavy flirting

Making a move

Shame Junction

More drinking

Crying

"I'm going to be alone forever"

Drunk texts

Masturbation

Shady Bay

Singing along to Journey songs

"Let's drink more"

Disgusting Bathroom Lane

Bum a cigarette outside

Photobooth

Drunk Food Plaza

INDECISION CIRCLE

"The next place will be better."

Vomitville

Long lines and cover charges

"Why am I at a club?"

"Um, yeah I guess I'll try some drugs."

Guilt River

"Screw it, I'll just dance"

Uber of indignity

"I am not a good dancer am I"

27

OPEN BARS

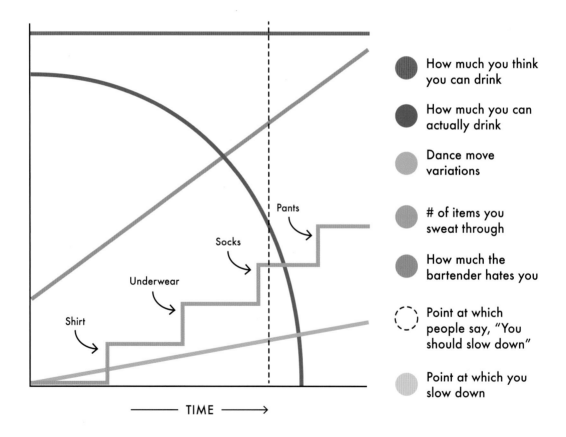

- How much you think you can drink
- How much you can actually drink
- Dance move variations
- # of items you sweat through
- How much the bartender hates you
- Point at which people say, "You should slow down"
- Point at which you slow down

Shirt

Underwear

Socks

Pants

TIME

VACATIONING IN THE U.S.

Where you go to see nature

Where you go to see city

Where you go if you're rich

Where you go if you're poor

Where you go if you want a tan (or are elderly)

Where you go to visit relatives

Where you go to sin

Where you go because your family just goes there for some reason

Where you go on the way to somewhere better

Where you never go

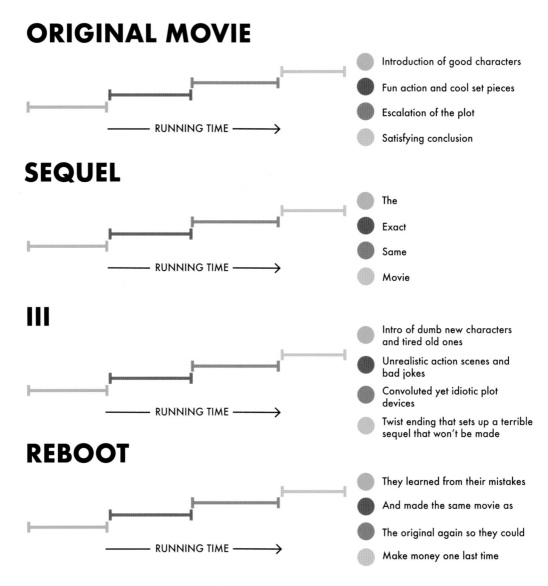

ORIGINAL MOVIE

RUNNING TIME

- Introduction of good characters
- Fun action and cool set pieces
- Escalation of the plot
- Satisfying conclusion

SEQUEL

RUNNING TIME

- The
- Exact
- Same
- Movie

III

RUNNING TIME

- Intro of dumb new characters and tired old ones
- Unrealistic action scenes and bad jokes
- Convoluted yet idiotic plot devices
- Twist ending that sets up a terrible sequel that won't be made

REBOOT

RUNNING TIME

- They learned from their mistakes
- And made the same movie as
- The original again so they could
- Make money one last time

WEEKEND SCHEDULE

SAT

SUN

 Watch TV

 Argue about what to watch on TV

Go outside in your bathrobe and peer into the sun like a crazy person

Run one errand

Poison body with food and alcohol

 Hangover

 Existential dread

Try to come up with a good excuse not to go to work this week

WHY I'M POLITE TO WAITERS

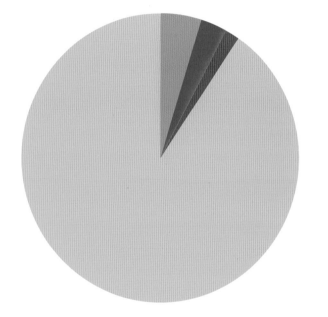

 Because they might spit in my food

 Because they might give me a discount

 Because they might go on a date with me

Because I realize they're just human beings trying to make a living, not my servants

USING SOCIAL MEDIA

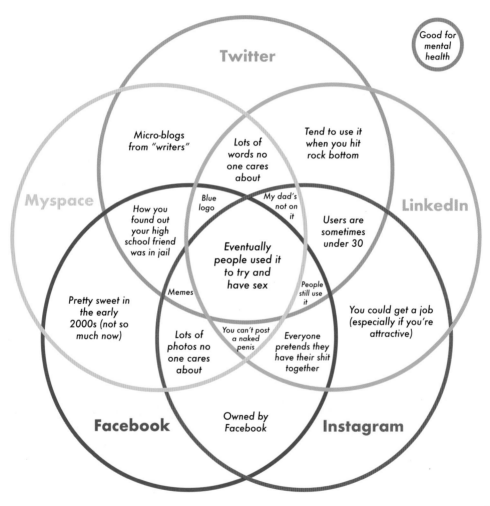

Twitter

Good for mental health

Micro-blogs from "writers"

Lots of words no one cares about

Tend to use it when you hit rock bottom

Myspace

Blue logo

My dad's not on it

LinkedIn

How you found out your high school friend was in jail

Users are sometimes under 30

Eventually people used it to try and have sex

Memes

People still use it

Pretty sweet in the early 2000s (not so much now)

You can't post a naked penis

You could get a job (especially if you're attractive)

Lots of photos no one cares about

Everyone pretends they have their shit together

Facebook

Owned by Facebook

Instagram

THINGS I DO IN MY FREE TIME

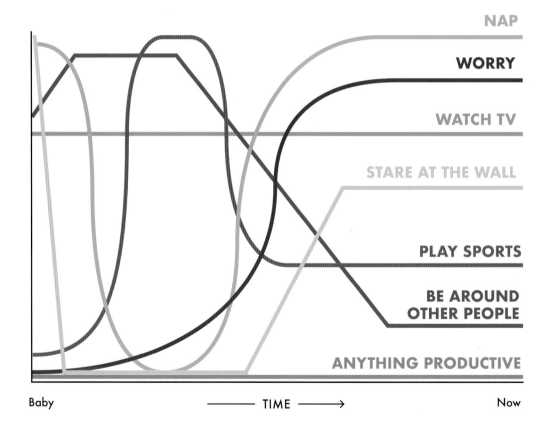

NAP

WORRY

WATCH TV

STARE AT THE WALL

PLAY SPORTS

BE AROUND OTHER PEOPLE

ANYTHING PRODUCTIVE

Baby

→ TIME →

Now

HOW TO DANCE WELL

DATING AND BREAKUPS

It's funny, breaking up has pretty much remained unchanged in the last hundred years. You either meet in person for an excruciating self-confidence bomb or just start ghosting someone and hope they forget you were ever seeing them in the first place.

Dating, on the other hand, has changed drastically, at least in the last twenty-five years I've been doing it. My first "relationship" was in seventh grade and lasted exactly one week, of which I talked to my new "girlfriend" exactly zero times. And I thought I was nailing it. Why risk screwing it up by, you know, speaking to them?

These days I know at least 10 percent more than I did back then. Nothing to do with keeping a healthy relationship going; no, can't say I know how to do that. But—I can pick out a hell of a first date spot.

FIRST DATE LOCATIONS

	PRO	CON
BAR	You get to drink	You're going to drink too much
RESTAURANT	Very classy	Very pricey
COFFEE	Cheap and casual	Goddamn how little are you trying right now
YOUR PLACE	You might have sex	There's no way they're coming to your place
THEIR PLACE	You might have sex	You might get murdered
GYM	N/A	It's weird you even considered this
HIKE	Conquering a common goal together	Ass sweat
BEACH	You're going to see them half-naked	They're going to see you half-naked
HELICOPTER RIDE	*sploosh*	You cannot afford a helicopter ride
YOUR OPEN MIC	You've rehearsed for this	You're going to be single forever

RELATIONSHIP CALENDAR

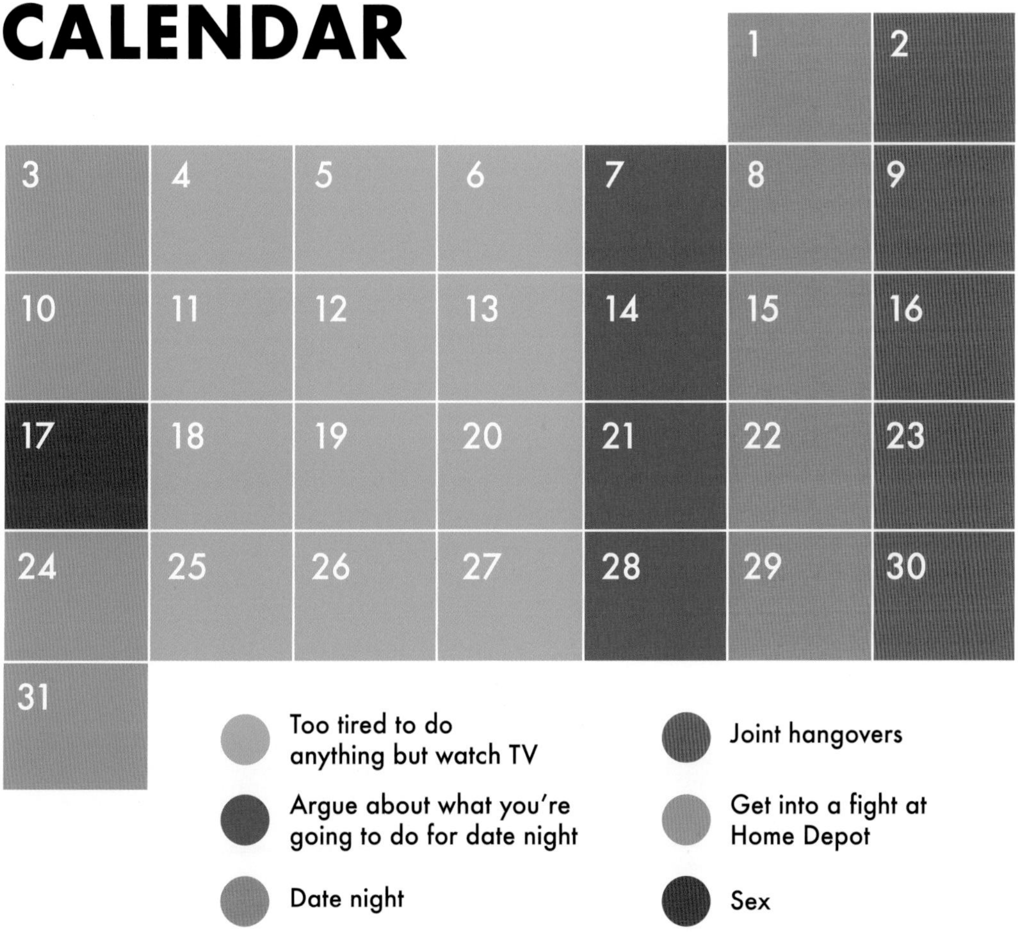

					1	2
3	4	5	6	7	8	9
10	11	12	13	14	15	16
17	18	19	20	21	22	23
24	25	26	27	28	29	30
31						

Too tired to do anything but watch TV

Argue about what you're going to do for date night

Date night

Joint hangovers

Get into a fight at Home Depot

Sex

SHOULD YOU ASK HER OUT?

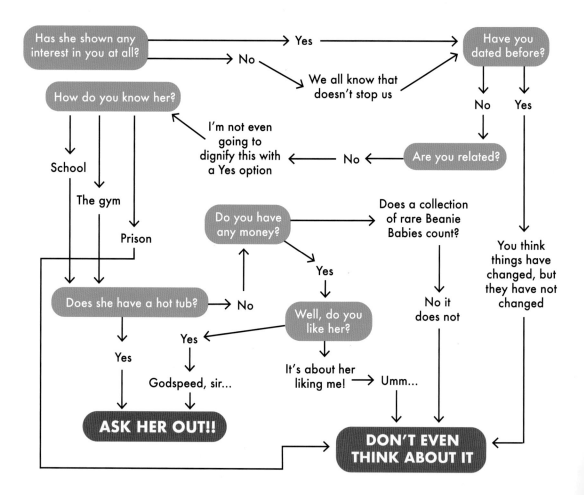

Has she shown any interest in you at all?

→ Yes ——————→ Have you dated before?

→ No ——→ We all know that doesn't stop us

How do you know her?

I'm not even going to dignify this with a Yes option ←— No ← Are you related?

Have you dated before? → No / Yes

School

The gym

Prison

Do you have any money? → Does a collection of rare Beanie Babies count?

Yes

No → Does she have a hot tub?

Well, do you like her?

No it does not

You think things have changed, but they have not changed

Yes

Yes ←

Godspeed, sir...

It's about her liking me! → Umm...

ASK HER OUT!!

DON'T EVEN THINK ABOUT IT

BREAKUP TRANSLATION GUIDE

BREAKUP LINE	TRANSLATION
I need space	I hate when we are in the same room
The passion is gone	I want to have sex with people who aren't you
We have different values	My family hates you
It's not you, it's me	I get all my dating advice from Seinfeld
Maybe we should take a break	I get all my dating advice from Friends
You're too good for me	I have done something horrible
I'm not looking for a relationship	You're not going to fall for this, are you?
You don't seem happy	I'm going to make this seem like your idea
I'm dying	I'm willing to fake my own death, that's how much I hate you

HOW TO ASK YOUR CRUSH OUT

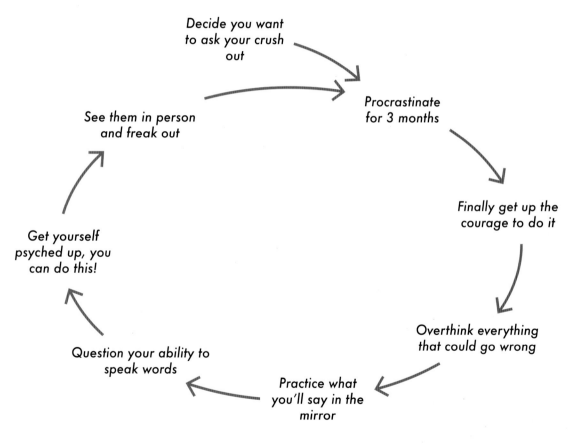

Decide you want to ask your crush out

Procrastinate for 3 months

Finally get up the courage to do it

Overthink everything that could go wrong

Practice what you'll say in the mirror

Question your ability to speak words

Get yourself psyched up, you can do this!

See them in person and freak out

FIRST DATES

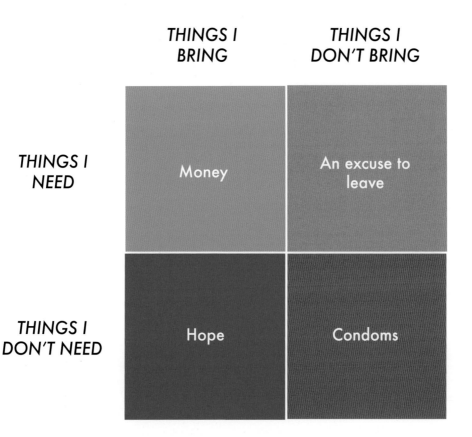

	THINGS I BRING	THINGS I DON'T BRING
THINGS I NEED	Money	An excuse to leave
THINGS I DON'T NEED	Hope	Condoms

BREAKING UP WITH SOMEONE

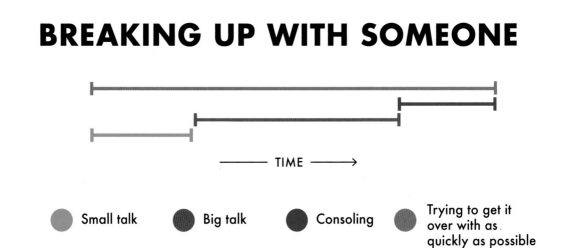

TIME →

● Small talk   ● Big talk   ● Consoling   ● Trying to get it over with as quickly as possible

GETTING BROKEN UP WITH

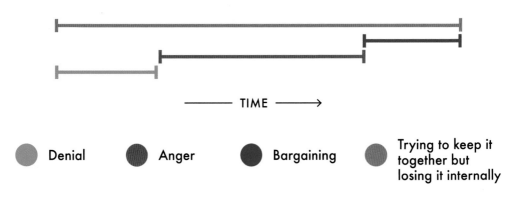

TIME →

● Denial   ● Anger   ● Bargaining   ● Trying to keep it together but losing it internally

COMMON GROUND

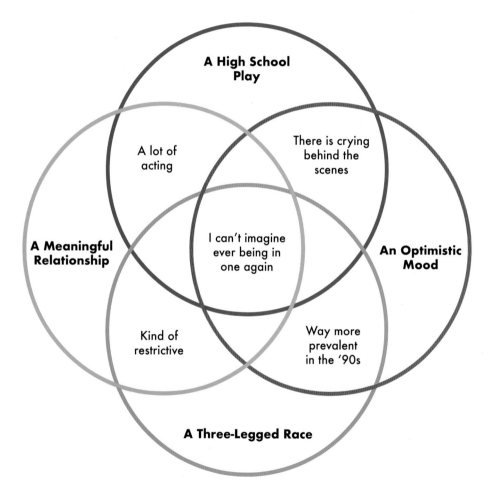

A High School Play

A lot of acting

There is crying behind the scenes

A Meaningful Relationship

I can't imagine ever being in one again

An Optimistic Mood

Kind of restrictive

Way more prevalent in the '90s

A Three-Legged Race

HITTING ON SOMEONE

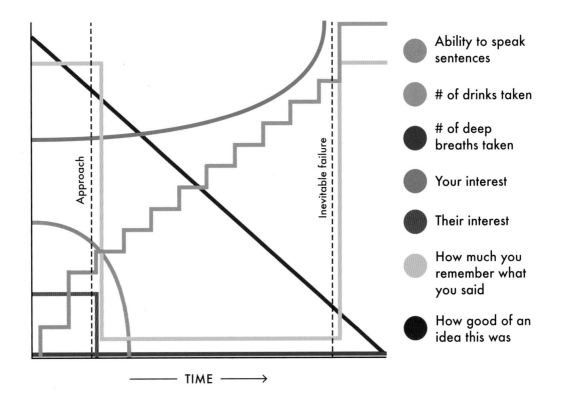

Approach

Inevitable failure

TIME →

- Ability to speak sentences
- # of drinks taken
- # of deep breaths taken
- Your interest
- Their interest
- How much you remember what you said
- How good of an idea this was

TINDER DATES

ATTRACTIVE

CAN HOLD A
CONVERSATION

WILL NOT
MURDER YOU

CHOOSE 2

RELATIONSHIPS
vs. MUSCLES

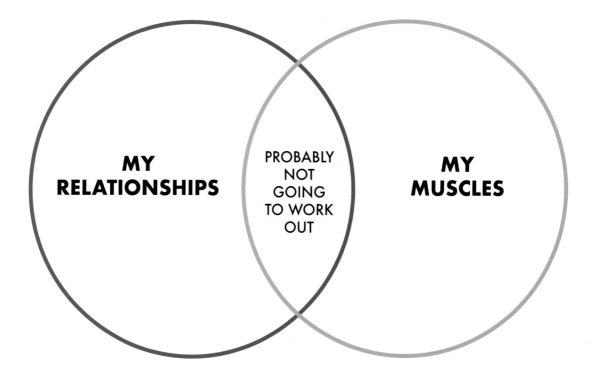

MY RELATIONSHIPS

PROBABLY NOT GOING TO WORK OUT

MY MUSCLES

SHOULD YOU DRINK ON THIS DATE?

Is the person you're on a date with cool?

YES

MAYBE

NO

Enjoying yourself? This calls for a...

Nothing cures indecision like a...

If you're going to get through this you're going to need to...

DRINK!

PARTNER HEAT MAP

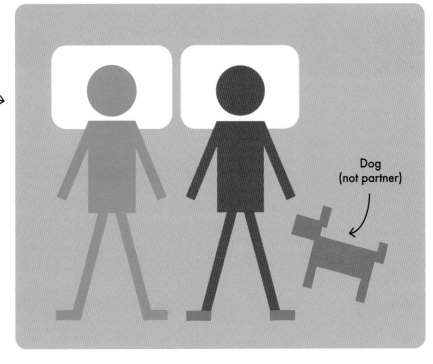

Bed

Dog
(not partner)

You: Cool, comfortable, 98.6°

Your partner's body: 5800° Kelvin, slightly hotter than the surface of the sun

Your partner's feet: -373°, a crisp Autumn day on Neptune

RELATIONSHIPS

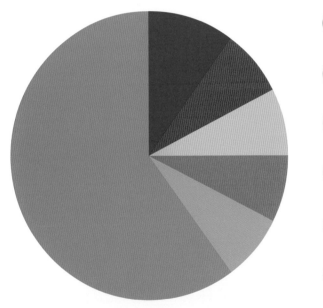

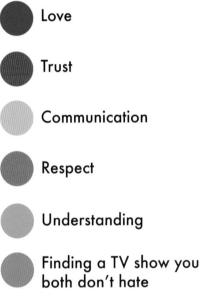

Love

Trust

Communication

Respect

Understanding

Finding a TV show you both don't hate

51

DATING, OVER THE YEARS

	HOW YOU ASK THEM OUT	WHERE YOU GO	HIGH/LOW	HOW IT TURNS OUT
ELEMENTARY SCHOOL	A friend of yours asks a friend of theirs	Lunch at the cafeteria	You don't say anything bad / You don't say anything	They break up with you on the bus ride home
HIGH SCHOOL	At a house party after 2.5 beers	The 7 o'clock showing of Clueless	You hold hands / You could not be sweatier	You date for 4 months and break up the day before prom
COLLEGE	At a frat party after 12.5 beers	Another frat party	They want to come back to your dorm / So they can eat your mac and cheese	You text them 109 times in 12 hours and that's a little too much for their taste
ADULTHOOD	Tinder	The nearest Applebee's	You kiss! / They say you are a bad kisser	You live happily ever after! Just kidding, you're alone forever

SEX

Originally I told my editor that this section of the book would be completely blank. Like you would open it up to a big title that just said SEX and then you would turn the page and it would be blank, and then you would turn the page again and it would go on to the next chapter. That's how it feels a lot of the time, at least in my world. Sex isn't something that's exactly relevant to everyday life. Sure, it's something we think about a great deal, but in the great pizza pie chart of life it's a slice fit for a supermodel.

But when I gave it a second thought, I realized that while it doesn't take up much of our time (especially the girls I do it with, ha-ha), it does leave a lasting impression on our psyches. Think about it: It's one of the most vulnerable things we do on this earth, which is why we are always second-guessing how we do it. It's quite annoying, really, and I for one am looking forward to a time and place in which I'm no longer interested in putting that thing there and moving around for a bit.

HAVING SEX

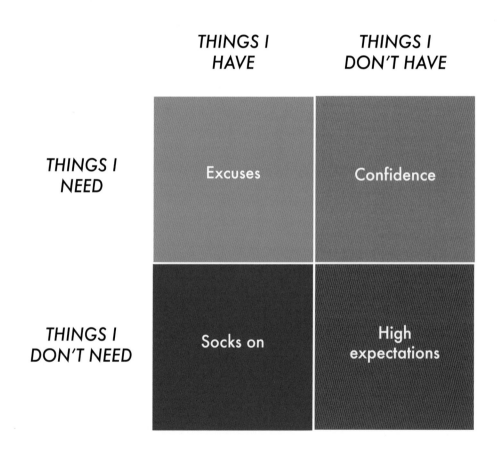

	THINGS I HAVE	THINGS I DON'T HAVE
THINGS I NEED	Excuses	Confidence
THINGS I DON'T NEED	Socks on	High expectations

FOREPLAY TRANSLATION GUIDE

FOREPLAY LINE	TRANSLATION
I'm going to slip into something more comfortable	I'm going to slip into something more uncomfortable
Should we get some mood light going?	Turn off the f–in' lights, idiot
I like it with the lights on	I am a sociopath
Should we get some mood music going?	I'm going to need a distraction here
I'm going to go freshen up	I really need to poop
We don't want to wake the neighbors	Shut up
Sorry I'm not feeling it right now	Wow you are bad at this
Do you smell something?	Do you smell?
Girl, you drive me crazy!	You're gonna hear, "This has never happened to me before" in about three minutes

THE SEXIEST CITY IN EVERY STATE

Humptulips

Heart Butte

Spray

Bliss

Rendezvous

Lovelock

South Rim

Aspen

Pleasure Point

North Pole

Chambers

Loving

Eden Roc

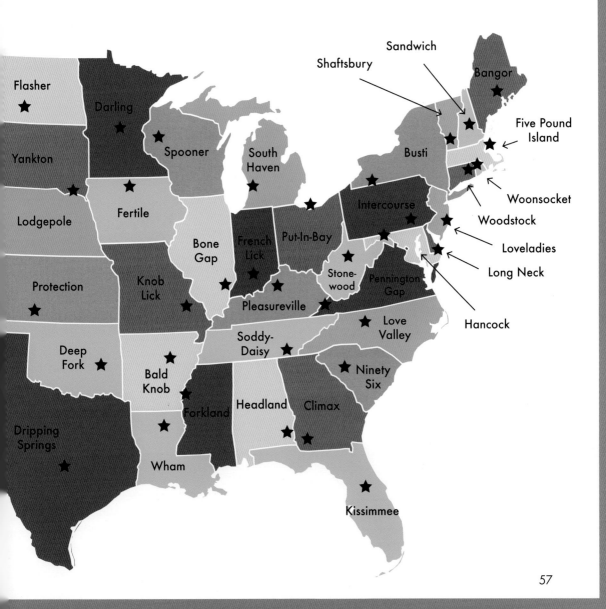

Flasher

Darling

Spooner

South Haven

Shaftsbury

Sandwich

Bangor

Five Pound Island

Yankton

Fertile

Busti

Woonsocket

Lodgepole

Bone Gap

French Lick

Put-In-Bay

Intercourse

Woodstock

Loveladies

Long Neck

Protection

Knob Lick

Pleasureville

Stone-wood

Pennington Gap

Hancock

Deep Fork

Bald Knob

Soddy-Daisy

Love Valley

Ninety Six

Dripping Springs

Forkland

Headland

Climax

Wham

Kissimmee

57

SEX POSITIONS

	EXCITING	DIFFICULT	SEXY	HAPPENS
MISSIONARY	X		X	
DOGGY	X			
GIRL ON TOP	X		X	
REVERSE COWGIRL	X	X	X	
WHEELBARROW	X	X		
SPOON	X		X	
STANDING	X	X		
BY MYSELF				X

58

THINGS I LOVE

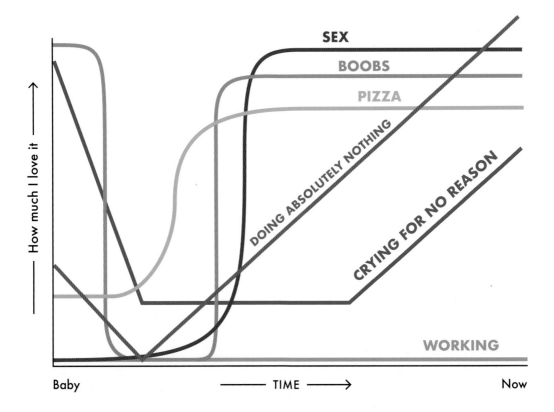

SEX

EXPECTATION

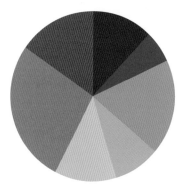

 Seduction

 Romantic mood lighting and music

Titillating foreplay

Yelps of passion

 Intense connection

Steady lovemaking

Mindblowing orgasms

REALITY

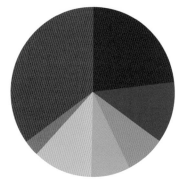

Apologizing

Fumbling to undress

 What is that smell?

Yelps of discomfort

 Sweating

Awkward thrusting

 Apologizing again

NETFLIX AND CHILL
(FROM YOUR DOG'S POINT OF VIEW)

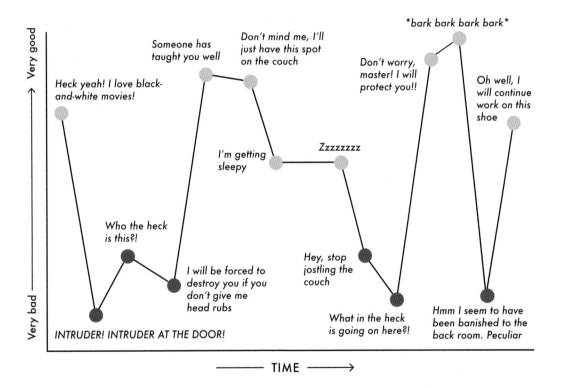

BAD SEX

B I N G O

They call it "copulation"	A metal song comes on	They call their mom right after	They call their mom during	A cat is there
They call you the wrong name	It's their ex's name	It's also your best friend's name	*Night Court* is on in the background	They lead a prayer beforehand
"My mom is going to be so proud"	They don't have a bed	**FREE SPACE** Someone throws up	It lasts 5 seconds	It lasts 5 hours
Photo of their mom next to the bed	They yell, "The Earth is flat!" during climax	Time doing sex < Time crying	They ask you to leave right after	They ask you to leave before
There's talk of a pyramid scheme	Their mom knocks on the door	They have their socks on	They ask you to sign their headboard	Chad is there

MY EXCITEMENT LEVEL vs. MY GIRLFRIEND'S SENTENCE

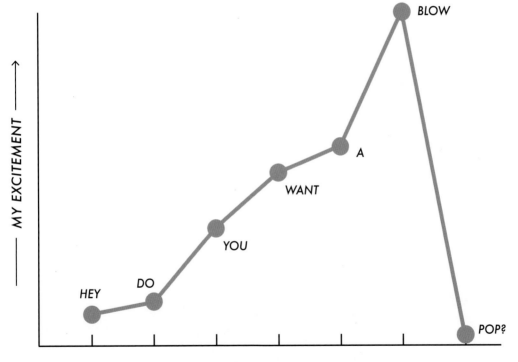

MY EXCITEMENT ⟶

MY GIRLFRIEND'S SENTENCE

HEY · DO · YOU · WANT · A · BLOW · POP?

THE BIGGEST LIES WE TELL AT THE DOCTOR'S

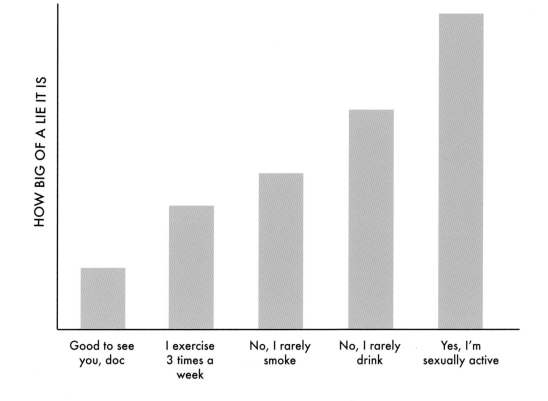

HOW BIG OF A LIE IT IS

Good to see you, doc | I exercise 3 times a week | No, I rarely smoke | No, I rarely drink | Yes, I'm sexually active

SEX TIMELINE

H

FAMILY

Like many of us, family is extremely important to me. It might be because I come from a large one, or maybe it's because said family grew up in tight quarters, pretty much only hanging out with each other. I remember my first day of preschool. It was probably the most terrified I've ever been. I didn't realize there were other people out there and when I was forced to interact with them, I retreated to the corner to hum to myself and play with my Playskool farm set like some kind of future serial killer.

But when I was around my family, I was a little more loose. Perhaps even too loose. As the youngest for seven years, I would often ask to be tied to a chair just so I could participate in the lives of my older brothers. And when I couldn't get free I would, predictably, start crying and get everyone in trouble.

Then my little brother finally came along and I suddenly became a middle child and started to take on middle child tendencies. I was no longer the focus of my parents so I needed to develop some shtick to stand out. What you're in the middle of reading right now was molded by that shtick. Thanks, family.

GUIDE TO SIBLINGS

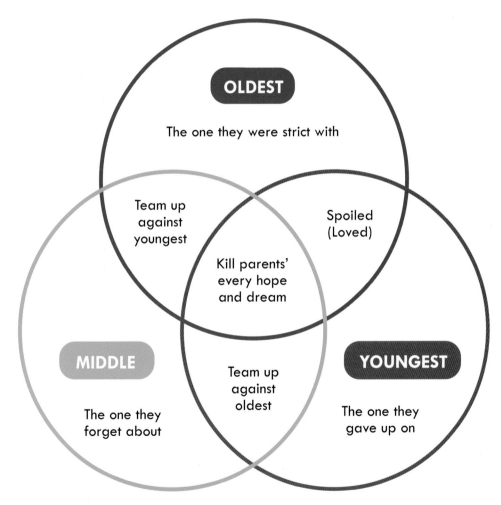

OLDEST

The one they were strict with

Team up against youngest

Spoiled (Loved)

Kill parents' every hope and dream

MIDDLE

Team up against oldest

YOUNGEST

The one they forget about

The one they gave up on

FAMILY VACATION CALENDAR

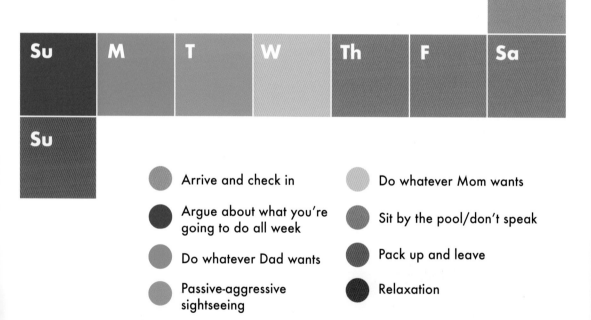

						Sa
Su	M	T	W	Th	F	Sa
Su						

- Arrive and check in
- Argue about what you're going to do all week
- Do whatever Dad wants
- Passive-aggressive sightseeing
- Do whatever Mom wants
- Sit by the pool/don't speak
- Pack up and leave
- Relaxation

TALKING TO YOUR PARENTS ON THE PHONE

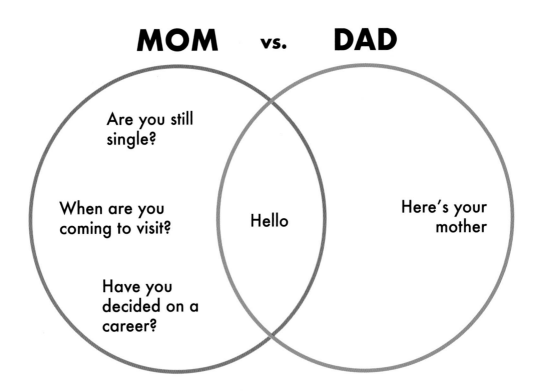

MOM vs. **DAD**

Are you still single?

When are you coming to visit?

Have you decided on a career?

Hello

Here's your mother

WHEN MY FAMILY GETS TOGETHER

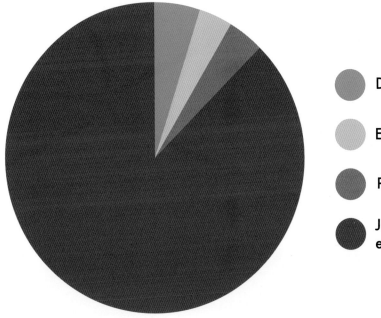

- Deep conversations
- Emotional debate
- Probing questions
- Jokes at each other's expense

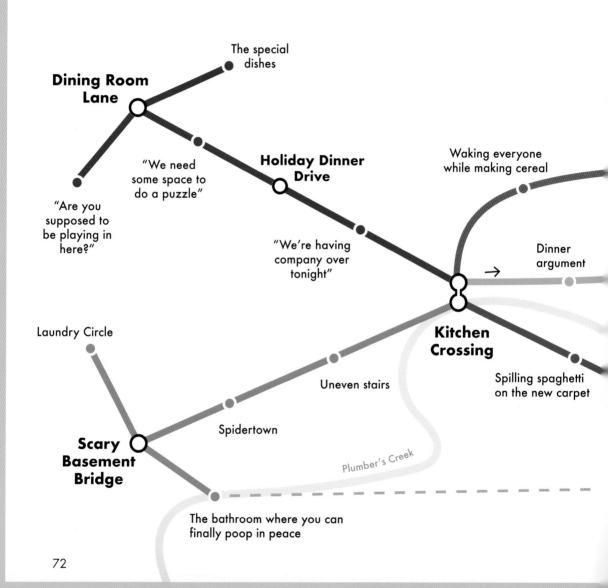

The special dishes

Dining Room Lane

"We need some space to do a puzzle"

"Are you supposed to be playing in here?"

Holiday Dinner Drive

Waking everyone while making cereal

"We're having company over tonight"

Dinner argument

→

Laundry Circle

Kitchen Crossing

Uneven stairs

Spilling spaghetti on the new carpet

Spidertown

Scary Basement Bridge

Plumber's Creek

The bathroom where you can finally poop in peace

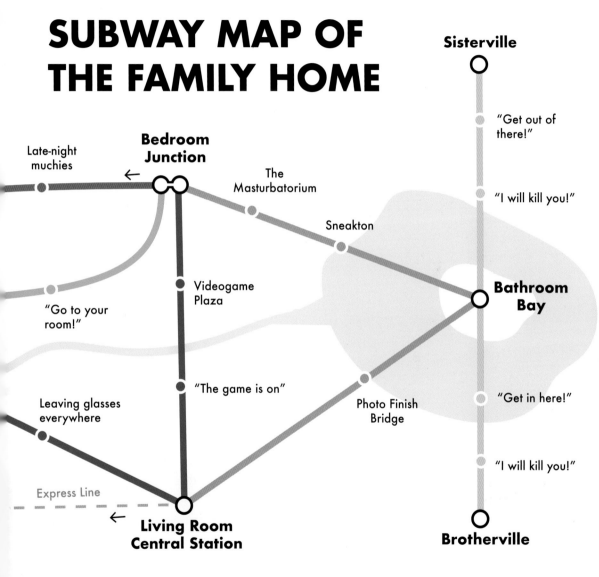

SUBWAY MAP OF THE FAMILY HOME

Sisterville

"Get out of there!"

"I will kill you!"

Late-night muchies

Bedroom Junction

The Masturbatorium

Sneakton

Bathroom Bay

Videogame Plaza

"Go to your room!"

"The game is on"

Photo Finish Bridge

"Get in here!"

Leaving glasses everywhere

"I will kill you!"

Express Line

Living Room Central Station

Brotherville

MY FATHER'S VIEWS

Things my father thinks are markers of a successful life

Things I've done

HOW WILL THIS HOLIDAY BE RUINED?

CHOOSE 1	+ CHOOSE 1	+ CHOOSE 1
Uncle Dale	gets drunk and fights	the dog
Cousin Mattie	tries to make out with	Aunt Janet
A gang of teens	vomits on	the turkey
The mailman	arm wrestles	the ghost in the attic
A mall Santa	falls in love with	Grandma
Your mom	throws mashed potatoes on	Uncle Dale
Your dad's girlfriend	rides	the TV
The cat	breaks a chair over	all of the decorations
Chad	can't stop laughing at	the family portrait
Your significant other	smokes weed with	Grandpa's remains
Everyone	murders	the baby toys

WATCHING A MOVIE WITH YOUR PARENTS

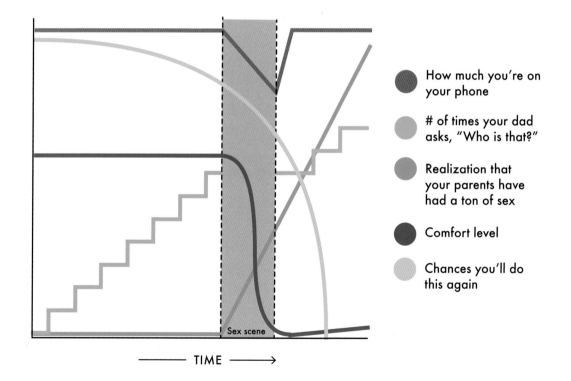

Sex scene

TIME

How much you're on your phone

# of times your dad asks, "Who is that?"

Realization that your parents have had a ton of sex

Comfort level

Chances you'll do this again

FAMILY GATHERINGS

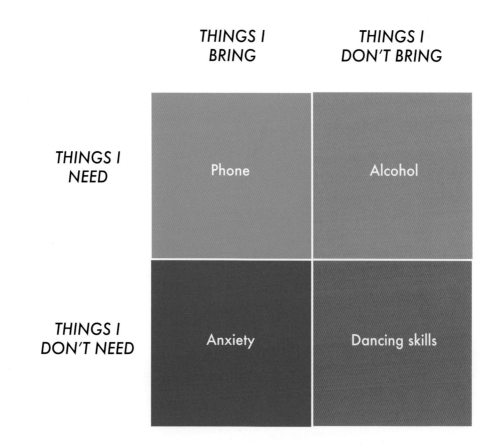

	THINGS I BRING	THINGS I DON'T BRING
THINGS I NEED	Phone	Alcohol
THINGS I DON'T NEED	Anxiety	Dancing skills

A DICTATOR vs. MY PARENTS

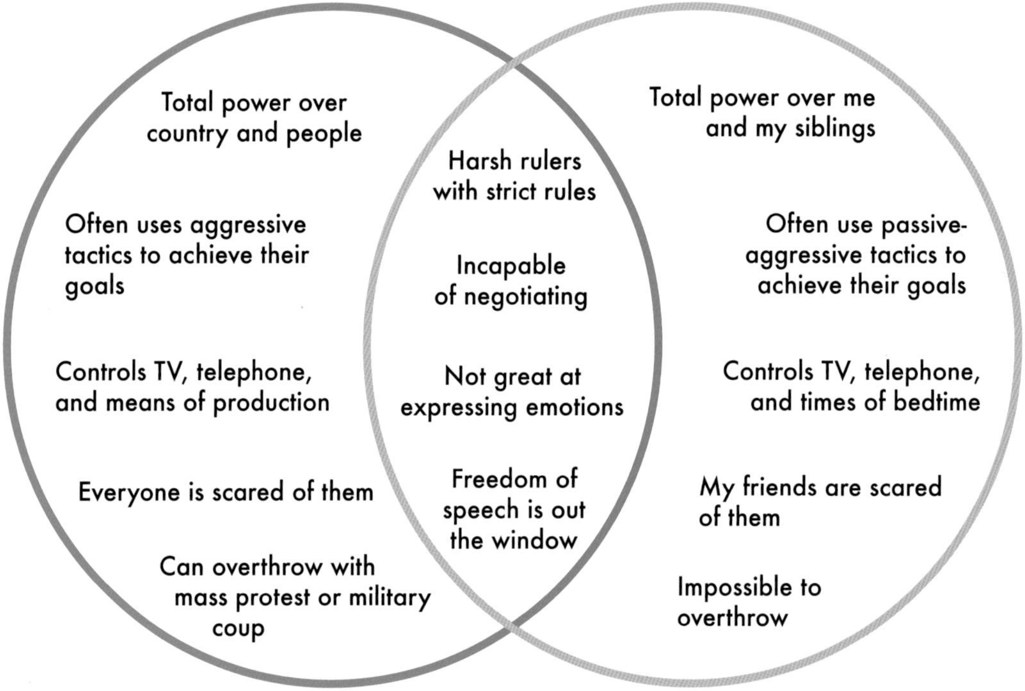
Total power over country and people
Often uses aggressive tactics to achieve their goals
Controls TV, telephone, and means of production
Everyone is scared of them
Can overthrow with mass protest or military coup
Harsh rulers with strict rules
Incapable of negotiating
Not great at expressing emotions
Freedom of speech is out the window
Total power over me and my siblings
Often use passive-aggressive tactics to achieve their goals
Controls TV, telephone, and times of bedtime
My friends are scared of them
Impossible to overthrow

MEETING YOUR SIGNIFICANT OTHER'S FAMILY

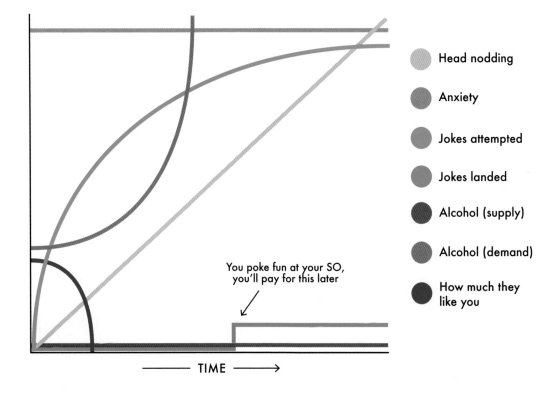

- Head nodding
- Anxiety
- Jokes attempted
- Jokes landed
- Alcohol (supply)
- Alcohol (demand)
- How much they like you

You poke fun at your SO, you'll pay for this later

TIME

EXTENDED FAMILY DINNER SEATING CHART

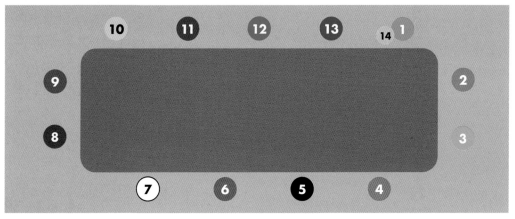

1. You
2. Uncle who brings up chemtrails
3. Uncle's new girlfriend who is always hammered
4. Someone's baby
5. Your much more successful sibling
6. Aunt who calls you by that sibling's name
7. Lady who you're not sure how you're related

8. Your mom who is pissed at your dad
9. Your dad who is oblivious
10. Grandma with the perfume
11. Grandpa with the inappropriate comments
12. Some guy
13. Cousin who repeats your jokes but louder
14. Your phone

HOW TO SURVIVE A FAMILY PARTY

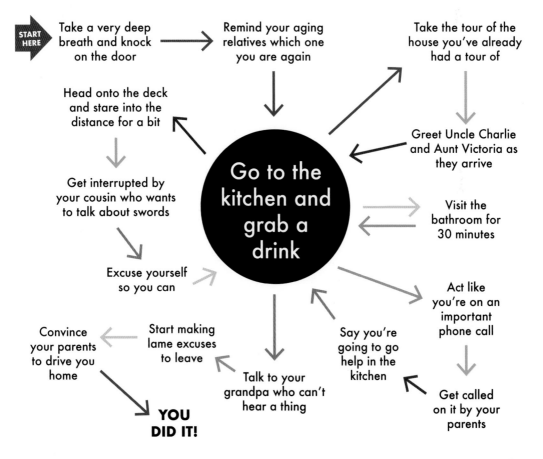

START HERE → Take a very deep breath and knock on the door → Remind your aging relatives which one you are again → Take the tour of the house you've already had a tour of → Greet Uncle Charlie and Aunt Victoria as they arrive

Go to the kitchen and grab a drink

Head onto the deck and stare into the distance for a bit → Get interrupted by your cousin who wants to talk about swords → Excuse yourself so you can

Visit the bathroom for 30 minutes

Act like you're on an important phone call → Get called on it by your parents → Say you're going to go help in the kitchen

Talk to your grandpa who can't hear a thing

Start making lame excuses to leave → Convince your parents to drive you home → **YOU DID IT!**

81

YOUR FAMILY

SUPPORTIVE

FUN

NOT INSANE

CHOOSE 2

FRIENDS

Making friends when you're a kid is relatively easy. Basically you look around for someone who is roughly your size and then start hanging out with them. Or if you're really brave, you simply ask, "Do you want to be friends?"

It doesn't really work like that as an adult. If I walked up to a tall, pale guy at the end of the bar and asked him if he wanted to be friends, I would probably get punched in the throat. Either that or it would work perfectly, but who has that kind of confidence?

Making friends is difficult, but keeping friends might be even more of a challenge. Everyone keeps moving away or having little versions of themselves. Why can't we just keep getting drunk in my basement for the rest of our lives? Are you telling me there's something more to existence than that??

Whatever, I'll see you all in twenty years when your kids leave the house and you want to drink in the basement again. Until then, I guess it's back to trying to make new friends.

MAKING NEW FRIENDS

EXPECTATION

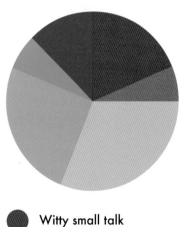

- Witty small talk
- A firm handshake
- Talking about the thing you have in common
- Connecting
- Exchanging numbers
- Plans to meet up

REALITY

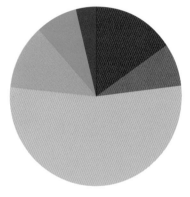

- Awkward small talk
- Why do you keep touching him?
- Talking about your high school knee injury
- Gushing
- He says he needs to go
- Looking him up on LinkedIn

AM I GOING TO GIVE YOU A HANDSHAKE OR A HUG?

WHICH ARE YOU GOING FOR?

Handshake

Hug

Then I'm going in for the
awkward hug

Then I'm going in for the
awkward handshake

I'M SO SORRY

WHY I GO TO PARTIES

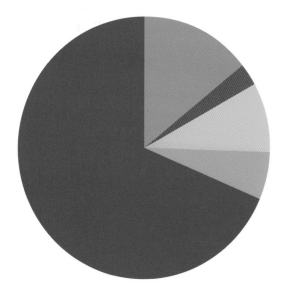

 Maybe there will be good alcohol

 Maybe there will be a cute girl to talk to

 Maybe there will be a dog to pet

 Maybe there will be a good movie on

 Maybe I will be the life of the party and everyone will do a slow clap and chant my name

 Guilt

F·R·I·E·N·D·S vs. MY FRIENDS

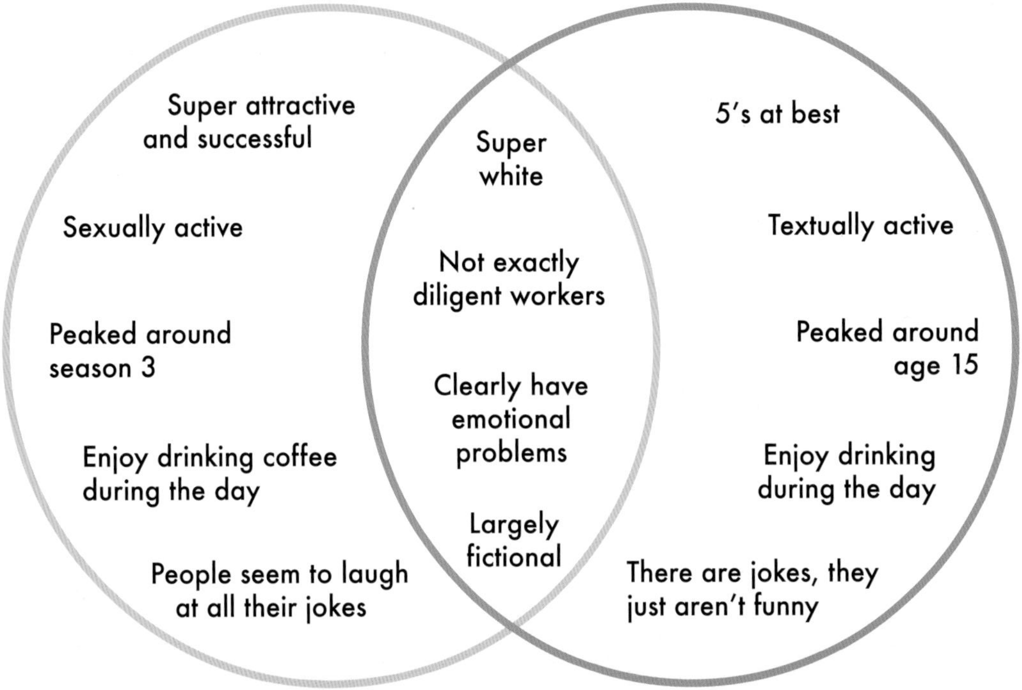
Super attractive and successful
Sexually active
Peaked around season 3
Enjoy drinking coffee during the day
People seem to laugh at all their jokes
Super white
Not exactly diligent workers
Clearly have emotional problems
Largely fictional
5's at best
Textually active
Peaked around age 15
Enjoy drinking during the day
There are jokes, they just aren't funny

WEEKLY DOG SCHEDULE

Su	M	T	W	Th	F	Sa

 Be your best friend

 Bark all day because you abandoned him at home and you're clearly never coming back

 Forget where he is and pee on the bookcase

 Chase the cat, then get beaten up by the cat

 Run away for 15 minutes

 Lose his mind when your parents show up

Sleep all day, it's been a long week

WEEKLY CAT SCHEDULE

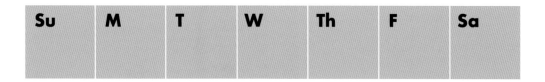

Su	M	T	W	Th	F	Sa

⬤ Not give a shit

GROUP TEXTS

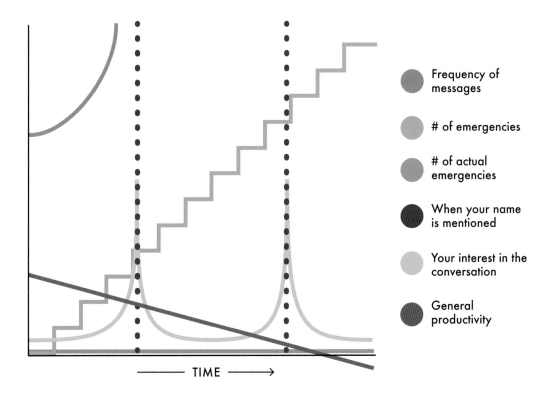

Frequency of messages

# of emergencies

# of actual emergencies

When your name is mentioned

Your interest in the conversation

General productivity

TIME →

EXCUSE TRANSLATOR

WHAT YOU SAY	WHAT YOU MEAN
Oh, the party was tonight?	It's rude that you reminded me of the party I was clearly avoiding
I'll be there in 10 minutes	I'll be there in 1 hour and 10 minutes
I just woke up from a nap	I was just masturbating
Sorry, my texts weren't going through	I have no respect for your intelligence
Who else is going?	Will a dog be there?
I'm not going to make it, I'm having car trouble	I'm not going to make it, I don't like you
Opps Id'b gto thdhd dhnkrrrn	Oops I got too drunk

PHONE CALL TIMELINE

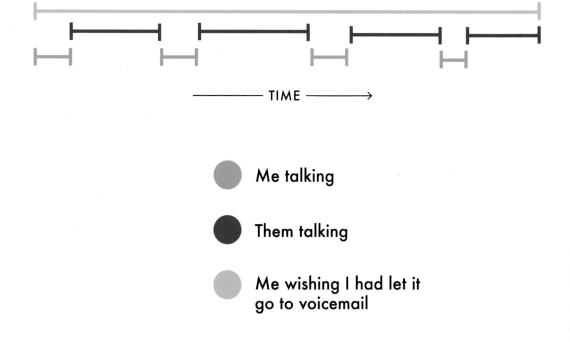

TIME →

○ Me talking

● Them talking

○ Me wishing I had let it
go to voicemail

ANXIETY, STRESS, AND OTHER EMOTIONS

I have another confession to make: I'm one of those people who goes to therapy and loves it. I'm sorry, I know it makes me sound like that one guy you hate, but it's helped me a lot with the anxiety, stress, and other emotions I've been wrestling with throughout adulthood.

You see, I didn't exactly grow up in one of those "sharing" households where people were open about their "feelings" and "communicated." I don't blame my parents for this, as it was how they were raised, too, but it has brought up certain issues that I've had to face as an adult, mainly how I relate to stress and anxiety.

I know I'm not alone when it comes to these emotions, and specifically when it comes to social anxiety. For some reason, we'd be more worried preparing for a house party than we would getting mauled by a bear. Our brains have turned on us and told us that we should be terrified of every encounter with another human being. I'm not convinced it has to be this way, but then again, I'm not convinced it doesn't have to either.

THE PERIODIC TABLE OF SOCIAL ANXIETY

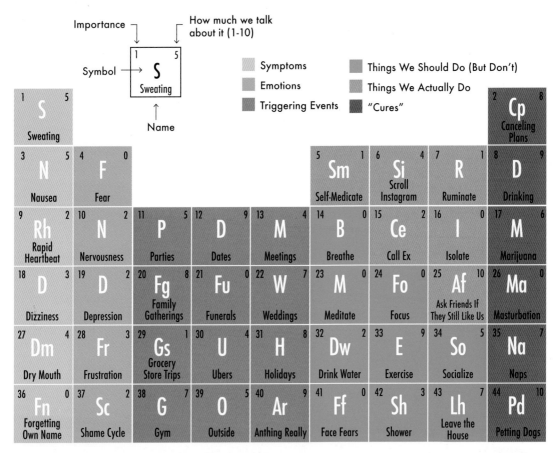

Importance
How much we talk about it (1-10)

1		5
	S	
	Sweating	

Symbol →

↑ Name

- Symptoms
- Emotions
- Triggering Events
- Things We Should Do (But Don't)
- Things We Actually Do
- "Cures"

1 — S (5) Sweating	4 — F (0) Fear						5 — Sm (1) Self-Medicate	6 — Si (4) Scroll Instagram	7 — R (1) Ruminate	8 — D (9) Drinking
3 — N (5) Nausea										2 — Cp (8) Canceling Plans
9 — Rh (2) Rapid Heartbeat	10 — N (2) Nervousness	11 — P (5) Parties	12 — D (9) Dates	13 — M (4) Meetings	14 — B (0) Breathe	15 — Ce (2) Call Ex	16 — I (0) Isolate	17 — M (6) Marijuana		
18 — D (3) Dizziness	19 — D (2) Depression	20 — Fg (8) Family Gatherings	21 — Fu (0) Funerals	22 — W (7) Weddings	23 — M (0) Meditate	24 — Fo (0) Focus	25 — Af (10) Ask Friends If They Still Like Us	26 — Ma (0) Masturbation		
27 — Dm (4) Dry Mouth	28 — Fr (3) Frustration	29 — Gs (1) Grocery Store Trips	30 — U (4) Ubers	31 — H (8) Holidays	32 — Dw (2) Drink Water	33 — E (9) Exercise	34 — So (5) Socialize	35 — Na (7) Naps		
36 — Fn (0) Forgetting Own Name	37 — Sc (2) Shame Cycle	38 — G (7) Gym	39 — O (5) Outside	40 — Ar (9) Anthing Really	41 — Ff (0) Face Fears	42 — Sh (3) Shower	43 — Lh (7) Leave the House	44 — Pd (10) Petting Dogs		

WHY I'M STARING OFF INTO SPACE

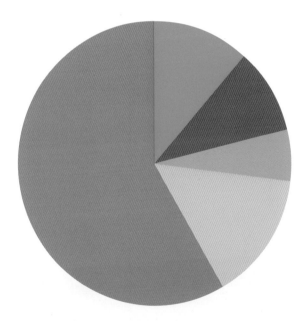

 I am pondering my insignificance

 I am daydreaming about pizza

 I am trying to do math

 I am being super present in this exact moment

 I am drunk

 I am overwhelmed by living life

SYMPTOM TRACKER

	FLU	COLD	ALLERGIES	BEING ALIVE THESE DAYS
FEVER	large	small		small
COUGH	medium	medium	medium	small
ACHES AND PAINS	medium	small	medium	large
DIARRHEA	large			medium
SHALLOW BREATHING	medium	small	medium	medium
INCREASED HEART RATE	small			large
WATERY EYES		medium	large	large*
FATIGUE	medium	small	small	large
SWEATING	medium	small	small	large
SENSE OF IMPENDING DOOM	medium		small	large

*Crying

96

STRESS AS AN ADULT

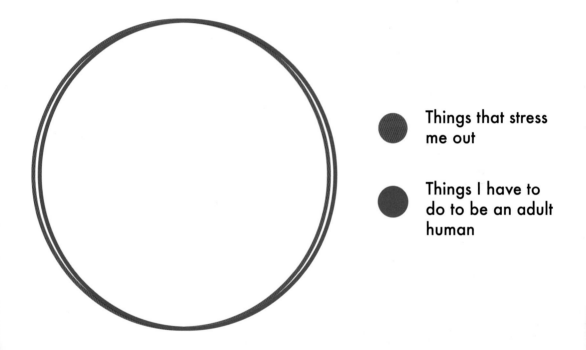

● Things that stress me out

● Things I have to do to be an adult human

TERRIBLE COPING MECHANISMS
WHEEL OF CHANCE!

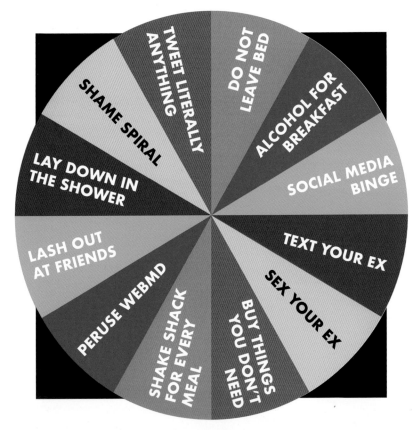

Step up and give it a spin!

TWEET LITERALLY ANYTHING

DO NOT LEAVE BED

SHAME SPIRAL

ALCOHOL FOR BREAKFAST

LAY DOWN IN THE SHOWER

SOCIAL MEDIA BINGE

LASH OUT AT FRIENDS

TEXT YOUR EX

PERUSE WEBMD

SEX YOUR EX

SHAKE SHACK FOR EVERY MEAL

BUY THINGS YOU DON'T NEED

SOCIAL ANXIETY

EVENT	EXPECTATION	REALITY
Leaving the house	Someone catches you off guard and you forget how to speak	You speak just fine
Saying hi to a stranger	They go home and make fun of you to all their friends	They say hi back
Going to a party	Everyone will notice you're awkward and don't have much to say	Nobody gives a shit
Petting someone's dog	You get in trouble for trying to pet a dog that's not yours	You pet the dog
Giving a compliment	They tell their significant other about the creepy person in line	They give you one back
Making a joke	Everyone laughs at you	Everyone laughs at your joke
Hitting on someone	They post on Twitter about how some ugly, lame person tried to talk to them	Okay they probably will reject you but you know what? That's okay

THE INTERNET

KEEP UP WITH
CURRENT EVENTS

KEEP IN
TOUCH WITH
FRIENDS AND
FAMILY

CHOOSE 2

KEEP YOUR
SANITY

HOW TO FALL ASLEEP

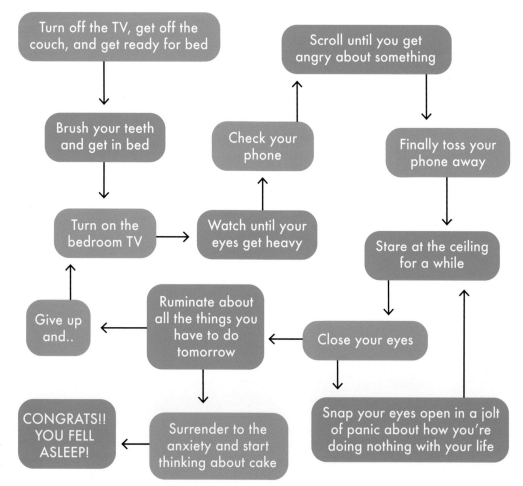

HOW STRESSED ARE YOU?

STRESS LEVEL	WHAT YOU ARE DOING
0	This has never happened before so you're probably in bed dreaming
1	Vacation, and not one of those where you have to do something
2	You just exercised and are currently sitting in your own filth, content but vowing to never do that again
3	You're drunk but trying to not get too drunk
4	This is your default, so you're just living life on a typical day of chaos
5	You're too drunk and trying to become less drunk by chugging water and clutching the walls
6	You're speaking in a work meeting, wondering if everyone else can tell how anxious you feel
7	You're laying down in the shower
8	Full on panic attack, trying to maintain a grasp on reality while on the phone with your mom

HAVING A PANIC ATTACK

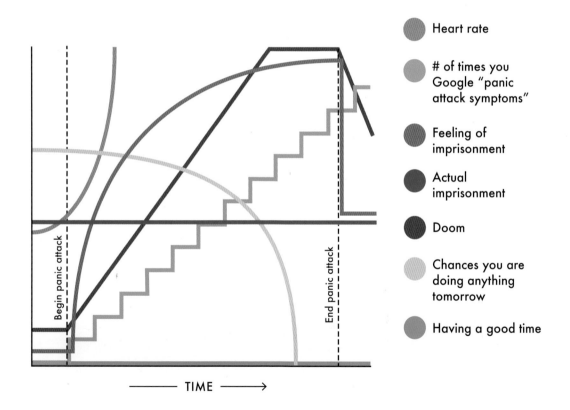

Heart rate

# of times you Google "panic attack symptoms"

Feeling of imprisonment

Actual imprisonment

Doom

Chances you are doing anything tomorrow

Having a good time

Begin panic attack

End panic attack

→ TIME →

GROCERY LINE ANXIETIES

How anxious it makes me

In line | In line behind staring baby | In line and you realize you forgot something | That grocery divider thing | Waiting for cashier to bag items (should I help??) | REMOVE CARD NOW!!

WHAT WORRYING IS GOOD FOR

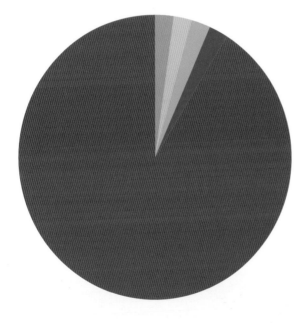

 Figuring out tough decisions

Learning from past mistakes

 Predicting what will happen next

 Creating an executable life plan

 Ruining your day

THINGS I GET STRESSED OUT ABOUT

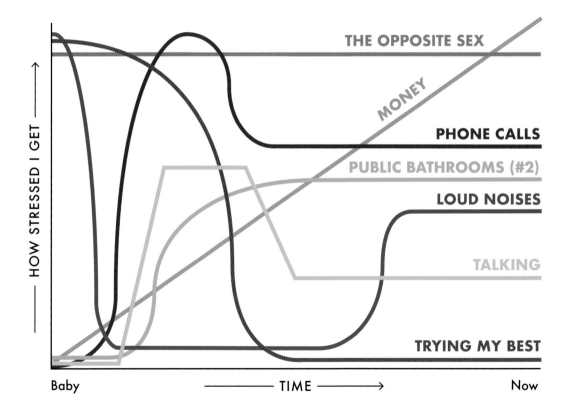

THE OPPOSITE SEX

MONEY

PHONE CALLS

PUBLIC BATHROOMS (#2)

LOUD NOISES

TALKING

TRYING MY BEST

HOW STRESSED I GET →

Baby → TIME → Now

THE 21ˢᵀ CENTURY BRAIN

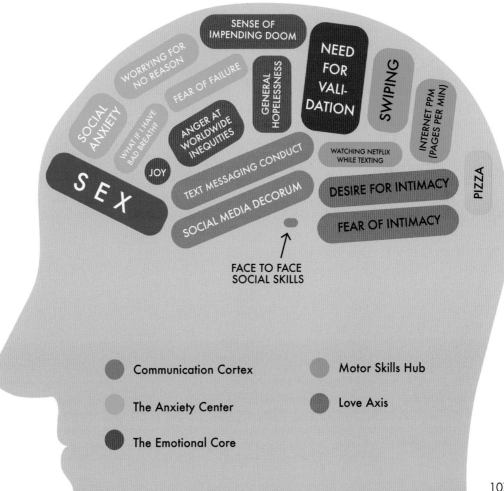

TAKING CARE OF YOURSELF

If you're like me, taking care of yourself is one of your last priorities. From doing laundry to working out to going to the doctor, these things just don't seem as important as things like, say, getting mad on the internet all day.

But I'm coming to realize that they are important. Not only do they keep you healthy and perhaps finally help attract a mate, they also give you something to do with all of the goddamn days there are in a year. I tend to find myself a lot happier when I'm *doing* things. Let me be clear: This realization has done little to change my behavior, but at least I can admit I know that doing little things around the house can lead to a happier Matt. Again, not doing it, but at least I know.

WORKING OUT

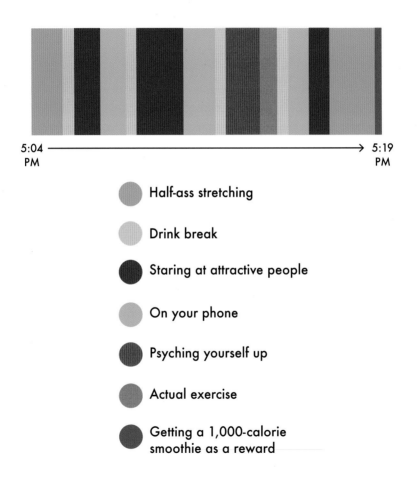

5:04 PM ──────────────→ 5:19 PM

- Half-ass stretching
- Drink break
- Staring at attractive people
- On your phone
- Psyching yourself up
- Actual exercise
- Getting a 1,000-calorie smoothie as a reward

DOCTOR APPOINTMENT TRANSLATION GUIDE

LINE	TRANSLATION
Good to see you!	I was planning on never seeing your dumb face again
I'm feeling pretty good	I think I'm dying
I'm just nervous I think	My blood pressure is consistently 240/170
Yes, 2 or 3 times a week	I haven't broken a sweat since 2007
No, only 2 or 3 times a week	I'm drunk right now
It started a week ago	It started a year and a half ago
I think it's my gall bladder	I have been on WebMD, can you tell?
Is there anything else we can do?	I would like drugs, please
I'll be back in a week to check in	I'm planning on never seeing your dumb face again

ONLINE RECIPES

EXPECTATION

 The recipe

REALITY

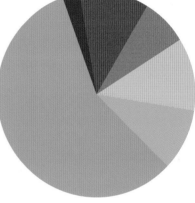

 Photos of the dish

The complete history of the dish

15-minute-long video of a random person making the dish

How the author was changed emotionally by the dish

Ads

The recipe

GOING FOR A RUN

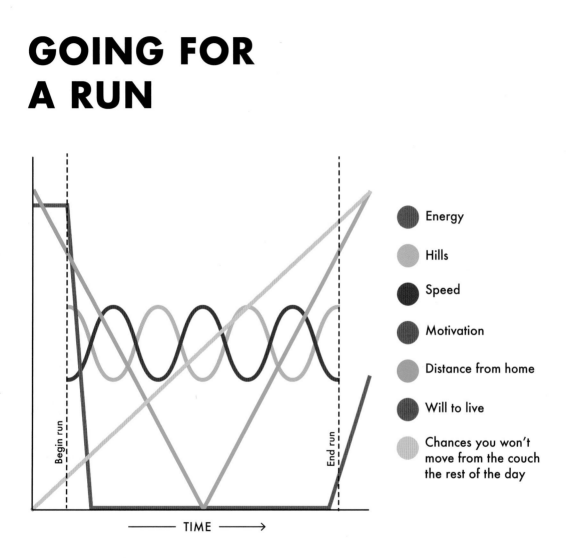

- Energy
- Hills
- Speed
- Motivation
- Distance from home
- Will to live
- Chances you won't move from the couch the rest of the day

Begin run

End run

TIME →

113

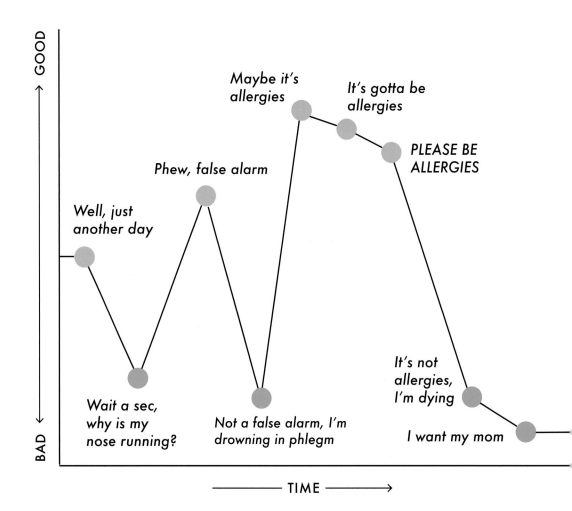

THE UPS AND DOWNS OF GETTING SICK

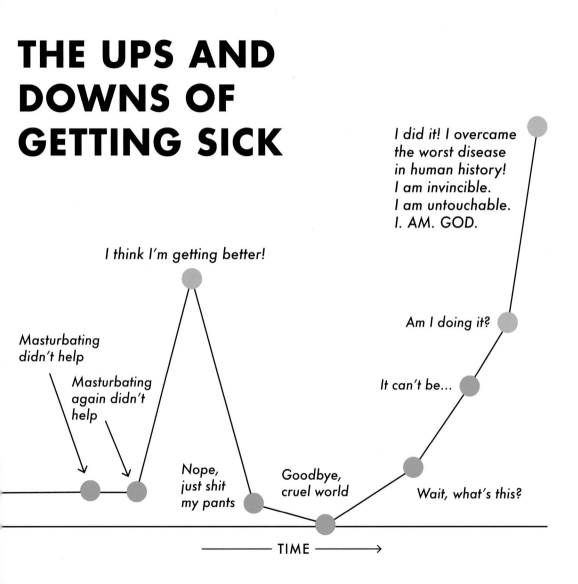

SOCKS OWNED

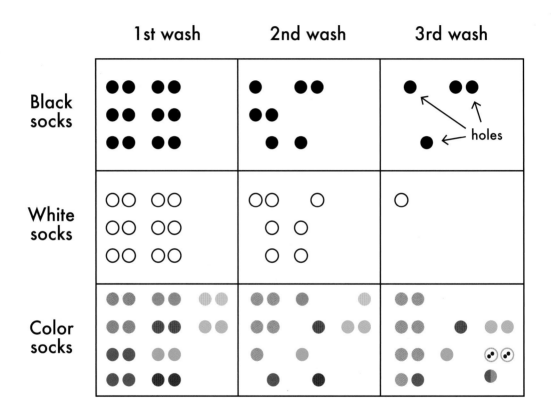

	1st wash	2nd wash	3rd wash
Black socks			
White socks			
Color socks			

holes

THE BIGGEST LIES WE TELL AT THE DENTIST

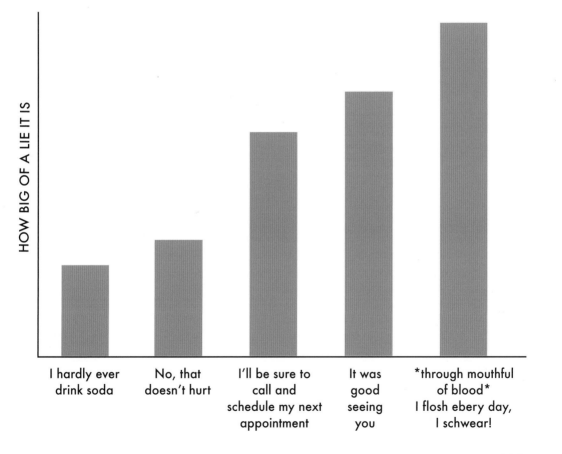

HOW TO MAKE BROWNIES

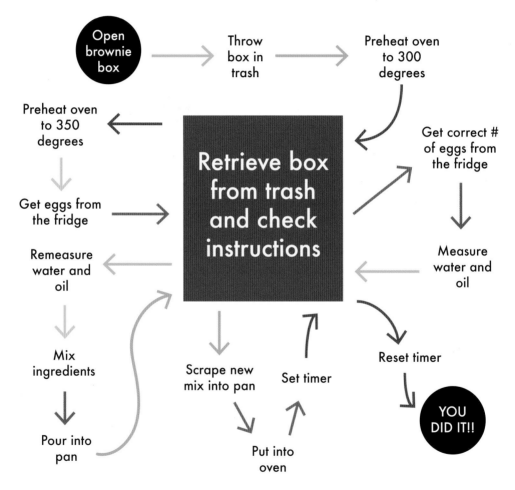

Open brownie box → Throw box in trash → Preheat oven to 300 degrees

Get correct # of eggs from the fridge

Measure water and oil

Retrieve box from trash and check instructions

Preheat oven to 350 degrees

Get eggs from the fridge

Remeasure water and oil

Mix ingredients

Pour into pan

Scrape new mix into pan

Put into oven

Set timer

Reset timer

YOU DID IT!!

TREADMILL SEATING CHART

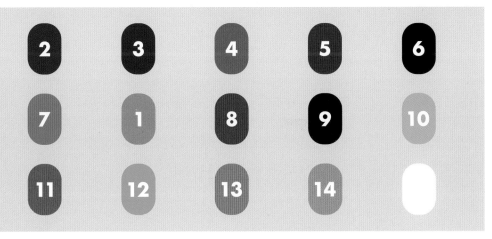

2	3	4	5	6
7	1	8	9	10
11	12	13	14	

1. You
2. Nose picker
3. Serial farter
4. Lady who is just watching TV
5. Instagram influencer
6. Guy who is losing his mind on an incline sprint
7. Fitness guru who has tips for you
8. Tween who is way, way faster than you
9. Drinking from a 2-gallon jug
10. Catcaller
11. Perpetually clearing her throat
12. Eating pasta somehow
13. Singing along to "It's Raining Men"
14. Person you think is cute
15. Person who thinks you are cute

CLEANING
THE HOUSE

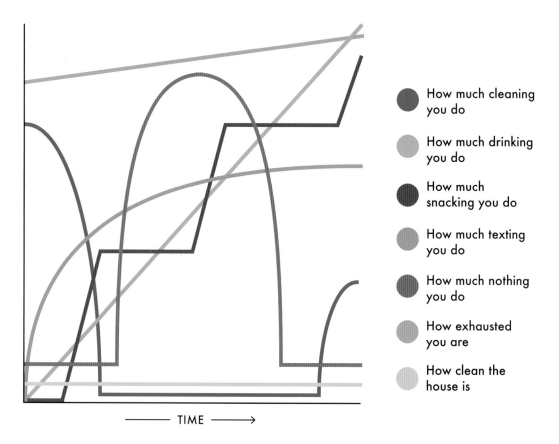

TIME

- How much cleaning you do
- How much drinking you do
- How much snacking you do
- How much texting you do
- How much nothing you do
- How exhausted you are
- How clean the house is

GOING TO SLEEP

WHAT YOU SHOULD DO	WHAT YOU ACTUALLY DO
Turn off all electronics before bedtime	Be on your phone until you doze off and hit yourself in the face with it
Wash your face, brush your teeth	Watch pornography
Make sure your phone is out of reach	Make sure your phone is under your pillow so radiowaves cook your brain as you sleep
Never eat in bed	Never not eat in bed
Read until you get sleepy	Cry until you get sleepy
Think happy thoughts while you drift off to sleep	Think of how much of a failure you are and get more and more anxious
If that doesn't work, count sheep	If that doesn't work, remember that time in 6th grade when you got dumped in front of the whole class?
Sleep soundly, accompanied by beautiful, vivid dreams	Sleep erratically, accompanied by caffeine-fueled nightmares

EATING HEALTHY WORD SEARCH

Find these words

DIET
VEGGIES
FIBER
PROTEIN
FRUITS
VITAMIN C
STRONG
BALANCED
HYDRATION
NUTS
CALORIES
MINERALS

```
S O M E O N E P S G D H C
L T E N A A R B Y I P A R
N J U P L E A S E R L O T
O S L N L L O T O O N R S
I L X G A L E T R L Y D E
T A I N N O E I E B O E I
A R C O L I E D R I S R G
R E C R N S R F O R X R G
D N T T V M E U F U E K E
Y I E S G I B S O M E X V
H M N S C N I M A T I V E
H S T I U R F F P I Z Z A
```

GROWING OLD

I contend that getting older isn't as bad as it seems. Sure, the one-day-closer-to-death thing is a little worrisome, but there's something about settling into the fact that you more or less know yourself that's comforting. You've seen it all before and you've lived through the best and worst of situations. It makes life a little less exciting, I'd say, but it also makes it a little more predictable.

On the other hand, predictability can be an unsettling concept. When we start up the car to take the same commute for the 10,155th time, sometimes we want to drive into a car wash with our windows open. This is perfectly normal. Life isn't easy, and the people who told us it was going to be when we were naïve little boys and girls should be disallowed from ever giving advice again. It's ups and downs all the way through until our last days when we, inevitably, download all our memories into an avatar and live forever in a sex utopia. But until then, let's take it day by day.

CYCLE OF ADULTHOOD

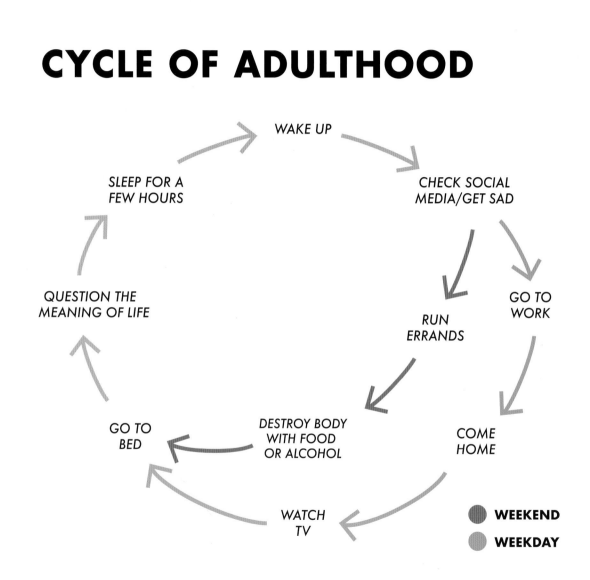

WAKE UP

CHECK SOCIAL MEDIA/GET SAD

SLEEP FOR A FEW HOURS

QUESTION THE MEANING OF LIFE

RUN ERRANDS

GO TO WORK

GO TO BED

DESTROY BODY WITH FOOD OR ALCOHOL

COME HOME

WATCH TV

● **WEEKEND**

● **WEEKDAY**

DRIVING, OVER THE YEARS

	WHAT'S IN YOUR CAR?	HOW GOOD YOU ARE	HOW GOOD YOU THINK YOU ARE	BIGGEST MISTAKE
HIGH SCHOOL	5 friends, some sports equipment, a whole lot of trash	Godawful	Amazing	Sideswiping the principal's van while trying to back into a space like a cool guy
COLLEGE	5 friends, some random clothes, a whole lot of alcohol	Bad	Great	Flipping your hatchback on the way to a first date
ADULT	5 kids, some sports equipment, a whole lot of tension	Mediocre	Mediocre	Switching lanes without signaling
ELDERLY PERSON	5 grandkids, a baseball bat, a whole lot of hard candy	Godawful	Who gives a shit	Taking a 10-minute drive through the mall

GROWING UP

WHAT THEY SOLD US	WHAT ACTUALLY HAPPENS
Secure that job you've always wanted	Continue that job you've always hated
Get married to the one you love	Get married to the one who can stand you
Enjoy the stability of a steady career	Get fired and dabble in pyramid schemes
Start a family	Start an addiction
Buy your first house	Buy your first couch at 30
Travel all over the world with your loved ones	Travel all over the county looking for aluminum cans to recycle
Get to know yourself inside and out	Gain 95 lbs, lose 40, then gain 60 more
Slip calmly into retirement	Slip calmly into a coma

YOUR BIRTHDAY (AS AN ADULT)

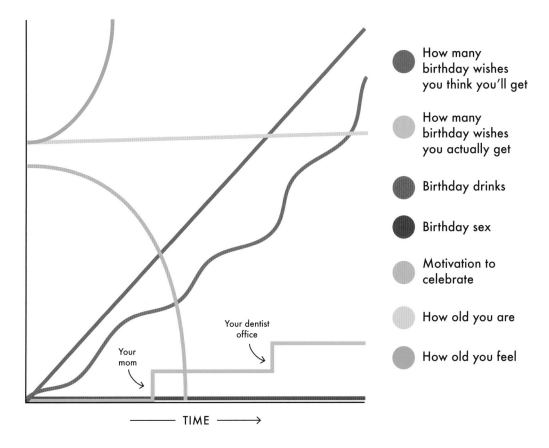

- How many birthday wishes you think you'll get
- How many birthday wishes you actually get
- Birthday drinks
- Birthday sex
- Motivation to celebrate
- How old you are
- How old you feel

Your mom

Your dentist office

TIME

BEING DRUNK VS. BEING OLD

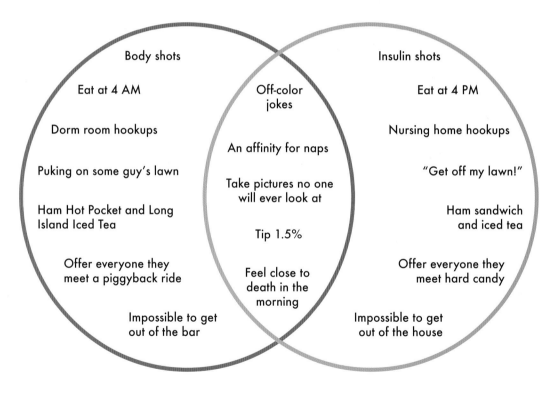

Body shots

Eat at 4 AM

Dorm room hookups

Puking on some guy's lawn

Ham Hot Pocket and Long Island Iced Tea

Offer everyone they meet a piggyback ride

Impossible to get out of the bar

Off-color jokes

An affinity for naps

Take pictures no one will ever look at

Tip 1.5%

Feel close to death in the morning

Insulin shots

Eat at 4 PM

Nursing home hookups

"Get off my lawn!"

Ham sandwich and iced tea

Offer everyone they meet hard candy

Impossible to get out of the house

WHAT'S IN THE BACK OF YOUR PANTRY?

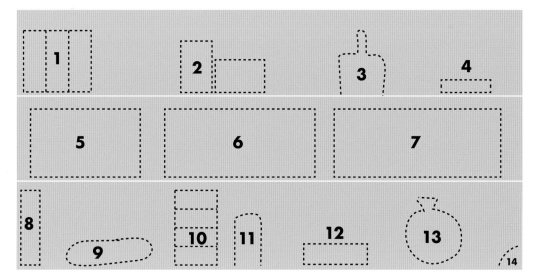

1. Cookbooks you've never used
2. Unopened bags of flour
3. Bottle of syrup you forgot about
4. One lone granola bar
5. Bags
6. More bags
7. Even more bags
8. Half a box of stale Cheerios
9. Marshmallows from 11 years ago
10. Matches, for some reason
11. Peanut jar with 3 peanuts left
12. Cookie tin you store old photos in
13. Halloween candy circa 1998
14. Your hopes and dreams

BAD HABITS TIMELINE

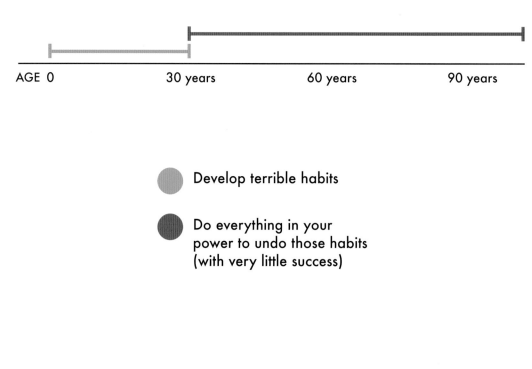

AGE 0   30 years   60 years   90 years

Develop terrible habits

Do everything in your power to undo those habits (with very little success)

ADULTING COSTS

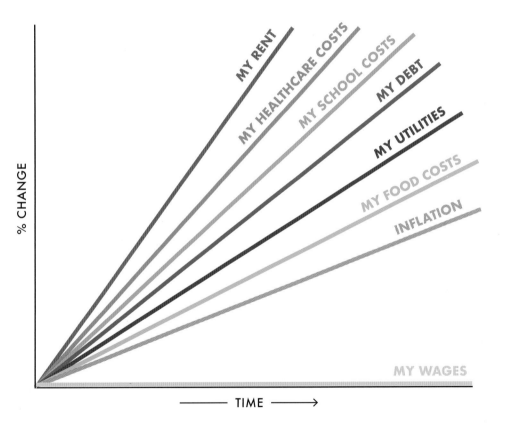

WHAT I THOUGHT I WAS SCARED OF

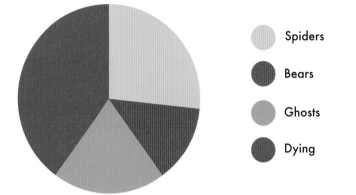

- Spiders
- Bears
- Ghosts
- Dying

WHAT I'M ACTUALLY SCARED OF

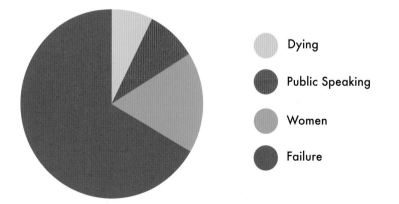

- Dying
- Public Speaking
- Women
- Failure

MY MAJOR LIFE REVELATIONS

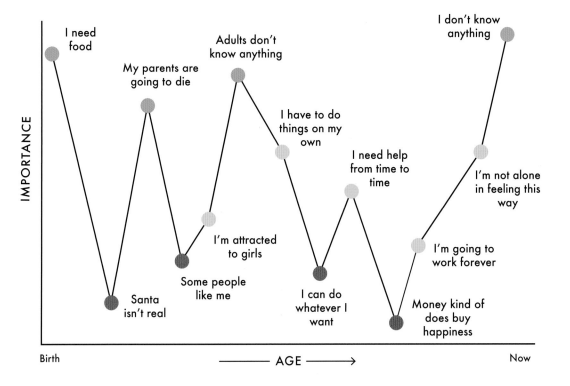

I need food

My parents are going to die

Adults don't know anything

I have to do things on my own

I don't know anything

I need help from time to time

I'm not alone in feeling this way

I'm attracted to girls

Some people like me

Santa isn't real

I can do whatever I want

I'm going to work forever

Money kind of does buy happiness

IMPORTANCE

Birth

AGE

Now

EVERY DAY TIMELINE

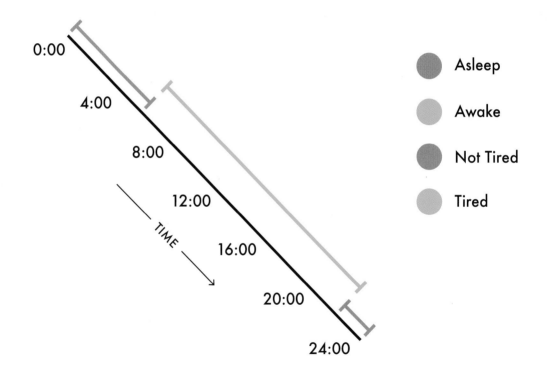

0:00

4:00

8:00

TIME

12:00

16:00

20:00

24:00

Asleep

Awake

Not Tired

Tired

THE OLDER YOU GET

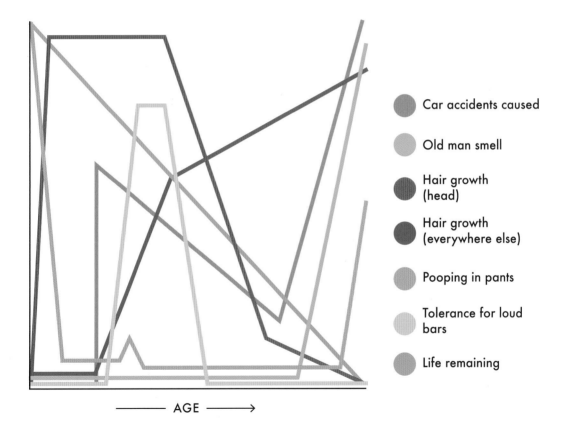

Car accidents caused

Old man smell

Hair growth
(head)

Hair growth
(everywhere else)

Pooping in pants

Tolerance for loud
bars

Life remaining

AGE

BEST (AND WORST) WAYS TO DIE

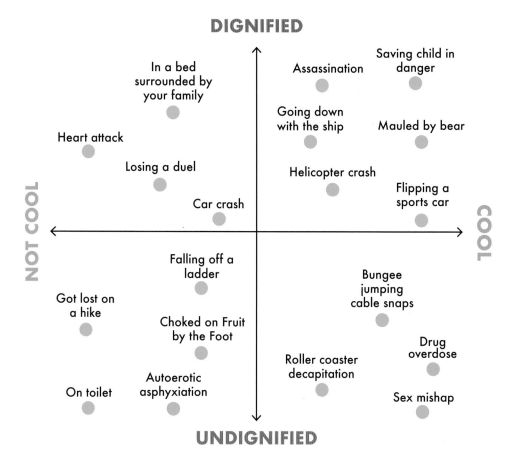

DIGNIFIED

In a bed surrounded by your family

Assassination

Saving child in danger

Heart attack

Losing a duel

Going down with the ship

Mauled by bear

Helicopter crash

Car crash

Flipping a sports car

NOT COOL

COOL

Falling off a ladder

Bungee jumping cable snaps

Got lost on a hike

Choked on Fruit by the Foot

Drug overdose

Roller coaster decapitation

On toilet

Autoerotic asphyxiation

Sex mishap

UNDIGNIFIED

THINGS I HAVE A LOT OF FOR NO REASON

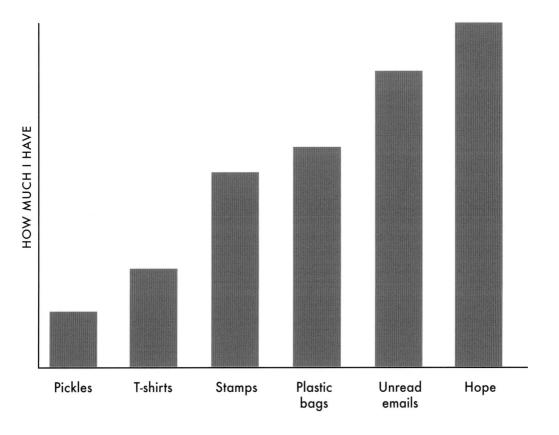

EVERY DAY TIMELINE

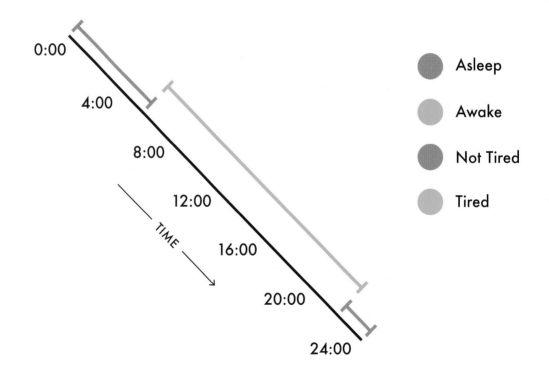

0:00

4:00

8:00

12:00

TIME →

16:00

20:00

24:00

Asleep

Awake

Not Tired

Tired

ACKNOWLEDGMENTS

Thanks to my fans and followers, for the inspiration, for the encouragement, and for correcting everything I've ever gotten wrong.

Thanks to my friends, for the inspiration, for the encouragement, and for listening to me complain about my fans and followers.

Thanks to Lilly, for the inspiration, for the encouragement, and for listening to me complain about my friends.

And thanks to my family, for being who they are.

ASK YOUR DOCTOR IF YOU MIGHT BE SHOWING EARLY SIGNS OF

ADULTHOOD
THE SILENT KILLER

KNOW THE SYMPTOMS:

1 The thought of waking up in the morning fills you with eternal dread

2 Sometimes you want people you don't know to fall down for no reason

3 Every time you can't open one of those plastic packages, you get an existential crisis

4 Anxiety that just won't quit

5 Canceling plans gives you a rush of adrenaline that's better than sex

6 Everything hurts always

7 You question the meaning of life every night before bed

TRY TO AVOID:

- AGING
- STRESS
- RELATIONSHIPS
- WORKING
- CHILDREN
- RESPONSIBILITY

POSSIBLE REMEDIES:

- ALCOHOL
- MALADOPTIVE COPING MECHANISMS
- OVEREATING
- AVOIDANCE
- ACTING LIKE A CHILD
- HIDING IN A CLOSET

"Adulthood is a common ailment, but with the right balance of depression and alcohol it can be treated and you can lead a sad, pathetic life." **—DR. ALAN PIERCE, M.D.**